e

MIKE OAKLEY was born and brought up in Dorset before moving to Bristol in the mid-1960s where he had a career in town and country planning until retirement in 1996. Mike's interest in the history and role of railway stations and halts in the evolving social and economic life of the South West led to the preparation and publication of a successful series of books, all of which were well received by local historians and railway enthusiasts.

Published by the Dovecote Press, the series was 'Discover Dorset' Railway Stations (2001), Somerset Railway Stations (2002), Gloucestershire Railway Stations (2003), Wiltshire Railway Stations (2004), Devon Railway Stations (2007) and Cornwall Railway Stations (2009).

Of particular interest is how station buildings and sites have changed over the years including the new uses where the stations have closed and clues to their former railway use. Reflecting this theme, the book Somerset Stations Then and Now was published in 2011. Mike has now returned to his 'home' county of Dorset and revisited over 70 stations and station sites he last visited in 1999/2000 when preparing the original 'Discover Dorset' book. This book is the result of the new research, including some 250 'then and now' illustrations and a schedule that sets out a short history and the current situation at all the sites.

DORSET STATIONS
Then and Now

MIKE OAKLEY

THE DOVECOTE PRESS

First published in 2016 by The Dovecote Press Ltd
Stanbridge, Wimborne Minster, Dorset BH21 4JD

ISBN 978-0-9929151-9-3
Text © Mike Oakley 2016
Photographs © Mike Oakley 2016 (also see Acknowledgements)

Mike Oakley has asserted his rights under the Copyright, Designs
and Patent Act 1988 to be identified as author of this work

Designed by The Dovecote Press
Printed and bound in India by Replika Press Pvt. Ltd.

All papers used by The Dovecote Press are natural,
recyclable products made from wood grown in sustainable,
well-managed forests

A CIP catalogue record for this book is available
from the British Library

1 3 5 7 9 8 6 4 2

CONTENTS

INTRODUCTION

Over the last fifteen years the author has researched the history, development and role of the railway stations and halts in South West England. This research led to the publication between 2001 and 2009 of a series of books on these stations and halts, each one relating to the region's historic counties. They included a short history of the county's passenger rail network, an account of the history and role of each station and halt and one or more historic photograph. During the research virtually every site was visited including those where all traces of the railway have now gone. Particular note was made of the current use of the railway buildings that survive, whether or not in railway use, and also the site where this was now in another use. Photographs of the then current situation were taken but very few were included in the books.

The first in this series of books *Discover Dorset – Railway Stations* was published in 2001. Site visits were undertaken over the period mid-1999 to mid-2000. The area covered was the geographical county of Dorset in the year 2000. Thus stations in the Bournemouth/Christchurch area were included but Yeovil Junction was not. The accounts of each station were in alphabetical order, the name being that used in the late 1930s except where the station had already closed. Where the term 'Halt' was included in the title it can be assumed that no facilities for the significant handling of goods were ever provided. The description of 'Up' and 'Down' platforms referred respectively to that used for travel towards or away from the London direction.

This new book up-dates the situation at the sites of the 74 railway stations and halts that have at one time or another existed in Dorset; today only 25 remain open including 5 on the reopened Swanage Railway. Photographs are included of the use of the buildings and sites when revisited in late 2015 and early 2016; alongside these recent new images are earlier historic photographs and captions noting the changes. Images are also included

Though 49 of Dorset's 74 stations have closed, evidence of their importance to the life of the county is still commemmorated. Here at Rodwell, the Rodwell Trail passes between the two platforms. The sign is one of those erected along the Trail to mark the location of the former stations.

of other features that indicate the former presence of stations even where there is now little or no trace of actual railway buildings, for instance public houses (eg. The Tap and Railway) or former station master's houses (eg. now called Old Station Cottage).

In some cases there is no feature to be photographed and these stations or halts are not included in the 'Then and Now' section of the book. However in the final section details of all Dorset's stations and halts are set out: the grid reference of the site; the opening and closing dates of passenger and goods facilities and a short description of the station/site history and 2015/2016 situation.

The book also includes a map illustrating the county's rail network and an account and schedule setting out details of its development and decline over nearly 170 years, 1847 – 2016.

DEVELOPMENT OF DORSET'S RAIL NETWORK

Railways came to Dorset relatively late in 1847 with the opening of the Southampton and Dorchester Railway. With a small population and little industrial or mining activity compared with many other parts of England, the early promoters of railway schemes saw scant evidence of revenue earning potential in the county. It is thus not surprising that the Southampton and Dorchester Railway was seen primarily as a section of a through route to Devon and the South West rather than as a new transport facility serving Dorset's residents and commerce.

Promoted by A. L. Castleman, a Wimborne solicitor, and linking with the London and Southampton Railway, the Southampton and Dorchester Railway (legally absorbed into the London and South Western Railway in 1848) provided Dorset with its first through rail link from London serving Wimborne and Wareham on route to Dorchester. The circuitous route, adopted to serve as many communities as possible, was given the nickname 'Castleman's Corkscrew'. The planned westward extension beyond Dorchester never materialised, this through route being provided to Exeter in 1869/1870 by the Salisbury and Exeter Railway which had opened through north Dorset in 1859/1860 serving Gillingham and Sherborne. Much time and effort had been spent in the rivalry between what were termed as the 'coastal' and 'central' routes.

The first north/south rail route into Dorset came with the opening of the Wilts, Somerset and Weymouth Railway in 1857 serving Yeovil, Maiden Newton, Dorchester and Weymouth. A second north/south route was completed in 1863 from Templecombe in Somerset to Wimborne, where it linked with the Southampton and Dorchester Railway. This line via Blandford was constructed in two stages: by the Dorset Central Railway from Wimborne to just south of Blandford in 1860 and then by the newly formed Somerset and Dorset Railway in 1863 through Blandford to a point north of Templecombe where it linked with the former Somerset Central Railway. The Dorset Central and Somerset Central Railways had amalgamated in September 1862 forming the famous Somerset and Dorset Railway. A further north-south line, the Salisbury and Dorset Junction Railway opened in 1866 from Alderbury Junction on the Romsey to Salisbury line south to West Moors on the Southampton and Dorchester Railway.

The other Dorset rail routes developed as a series of branch lines from the main lines: Southampton to Dorchester; Yeovil to Weymouth; Salisbury to Exeter. This was surprisingly the case with the Poole/Bournemouth area, the latter being only a small settlement at the start of the railway age. Poole was first served in 1847 by a short branch line to Hamworthy (and then by a short toll bridge or ferry crossing to Poole Quay). A more direct line into the town itself opened from Broadstone in 1872; both these lines branched from the Southampton to Dorchester Railway. The 1872 branch was extended into west Bournemouth in 1874 terminating at Bournemouth West station. Some four years earlier, rail lines entered the east side of Bournemouth as an extension of the 1862 Ringwood to Christchurch Railway terminating at the first Bournemouth station. The suffix East was added in 1874 with the opening of the West station.

There were significant developments in 1888: the opening of a new line through Bournemouth linking the two earlier lines that had penetrated the growing area from west and east and also, but not in Dorset, the direct line from Southampton to Bournemouth via Brockenhurst replacing the longer route via Ringwood. The final section in the development of the rail network in the Poole/Bournemouth area was the opening of the Holes Bay curve in 1893 linking Poole and Hamworthy Junction thus giving for the first time a direct route through Poole/Bournemouth from Southampton and London into Dorset replacing the earlier longer route though Ringwood and Wimborne.

The years 1857 to 1903 saw the following developments in Dorset's passenger rail network: Maiden Newton to Bridport (1857); Weymouth to Portland (1865); Wareham to Swanage and the Abbotsbury branch (both 1885);

Bridport to West Bay (1888); Weymouth Quay tramway (1889); Portland to Easton (1902); Axminster to Lyme Regis (1903). Short lived branches also opened to military camps at Blandford (1919-1921) and Bovington (1919-1928). The peak of the Dorset railway mileage of 170 miles was reached in 1920. Details of this evolution of the network are set out in the following schedule.

With the development of this rail network the pattern of life in Dorset changed for ever. Enhanced possibilities for travel and trading revolutionised life in the county's towns and villages. For the first time residents were able to travel easily to local and more distant destinations. For the rural communities there were easier movements of livestock and arable products; dairy farming in particular was boosted by the new opportunities for fast and reliable transport of milk to distant markets. Market towns served by the railways grew at the expense of those without. The tourism industry at Weymouth, Swanage and Bounemouth benefitted greatly from the new opportunities for visitors travelling long distances from London, the Midlands and North of England.

CHRONOLOGICAL DEVELOPMENT 1847 – 1995

1847
1st June. Opening of the Southampton – Ringwood – Wimborne – Wareham – Dorchester line (The Southampton and Dorchester Railway absorbed by the London and South Western Railway in 1848).
1st June. Opening of the Poole Junction (from 1872 Hamworthy Junction) to Poole (from 1872 Hamworthy) branch line from the Southampton and Dorchester Railway.

1857
20th January. Opening of the Yeovil – Maiden Newton – Dorchester section of the Wilts, Somerset and Weymouth Railway.
12th November. Opening of the Bridport Railway from Maiden Newton on the Yeovil – Dorchester line to Bridport.

1859
2nd May. Opening of the Salisbury – Gillingham section of the Salisbury and Yeovil Railway.

1860
7th May. Opening of the Gillingham – Sherborne section of the Salisbury and Yeovil Railway.
1st June. Opening of the Sherborne – Yeovil Junction section of the Salisbury and Yeovil Railway.
1st November. Opening of the Wimborne – Blandford St Mary section of the Dorset Central Railway.

1862
13th November. Opening of the Ringwood – Christchurch branch from the Southampton and Dorchester Railway.

1863
10th September. Opening of the Blandford St Mary – Blandford – Templecombe section of the Somerset and Dorset Railway (formal opening 31st August 1863).
1865
16th October. Opening of the Weymouth and Portland Railway.

1866
20th December. Opening of the Salisbury and Dorset Junction Railway from Alderbury Junction on the Romsey – Salisbury line to West Moors on the Southampton to Dorchester Railway, via Verwood.

1870
18th March. Opening of the Christchurch – Bournemouth (from 1874 Bournemouth East) line.

1872
2nd December. Opening of the New Poole Junction (later Broadstone) on the Southampton and Dorchester Railway to Poole branch.

1874
15th June. Opening of the Poole – Bournemouth West line.

1884
31st March. Opening of the Bridport – Bridport West Bay extension of the Bridport Railway.

1885
20th May. Opening of the Swanage Railway, Wareham – Corfe Castle –Swanage.
9th November. Opening of the Abbotsbury branch line from Upwey Junction on the Dorchester – Weymouth line

to Abbotsbury.

1886
5th March. Opening of the Corfe Mullen – Broadstone cut off line bypassing Wimborne for north – south passenger traffic, Blandford to Poole (opened for goods traffic 1885)

1888
5th March. Opening of the Bournemouth East (from 1893 Central) – Poole line.

1889
4th August. Opening to passenger traffic of the Weymouth Quay line (opened for goods traffic !6th October 1865).

1893
19th May. Opening of the Holes Bay curve linking Poole with Hamworthy Junction.

1896
1st July. Closure of the Hamworthy Junction to Hamworthy line to passenger traffic.

1902
1st September. Opening of the Portland - Easton line to passenger traffic (opened for goods traffic 1st October 1900).

1903
24th August. Opening of the Axminster and Lyme Regis Light Railway.

1930
22nd September. Closure of the Bridport – West Bay extension of the Bridport Railway to passenger traffic (remained open to goods traffic until 1962).

1936
Closure of the Corfe Mullen – Wimborne direct link.

1952
2nd March Closure of the Weymouth – Portland – Easton line to passenger traffic (remained open to goods traffic until 1965).
1st December. Closure to all traffic of the Upwey – Abbotsbury branch (short section to Upwey station remained open for goods traffic until 1st January 1962).

1964
4th May. Closure to passenger traffic of the Ringwood – Broadstone line. Goods trafic continued to operate between Poole and Ringwood until 1967, to West Moors until 1974 and to Wimborne until 1977.
4th May. Closure of the (Salisbury) - Alderbury Junction – West Moors line via Verwood.

1965
29th November. Closure of the Axminster – Lyme Regis branch.

1966
7th March. Closure to passenger traffic of the former Somerset and Dorset line Poole – Templecombe (between Broadstone and Blandford the line was retained for limited goods traffic until 1969).

1972
3rd January. Closure of the Swanage branch for passenger traffic (the section from Worgret Junction, near Wareham, to Furzebrook was retained initially to serve the clay works and subsequently the oil/gas developments).

1975
5th May. Closure of the Maiden Newton – Bridport line.

1984
Easter. Opening of Swanage – Herston Halt section of reopened Swanage Railway.

1989
March. Opening of Herston Halt – Harmans Cross section of reopened Swanage Railway.

1995
12th August. Opening of Harmans Cross – Corfe Castle – Norden section of the reopened Swanage Railway.

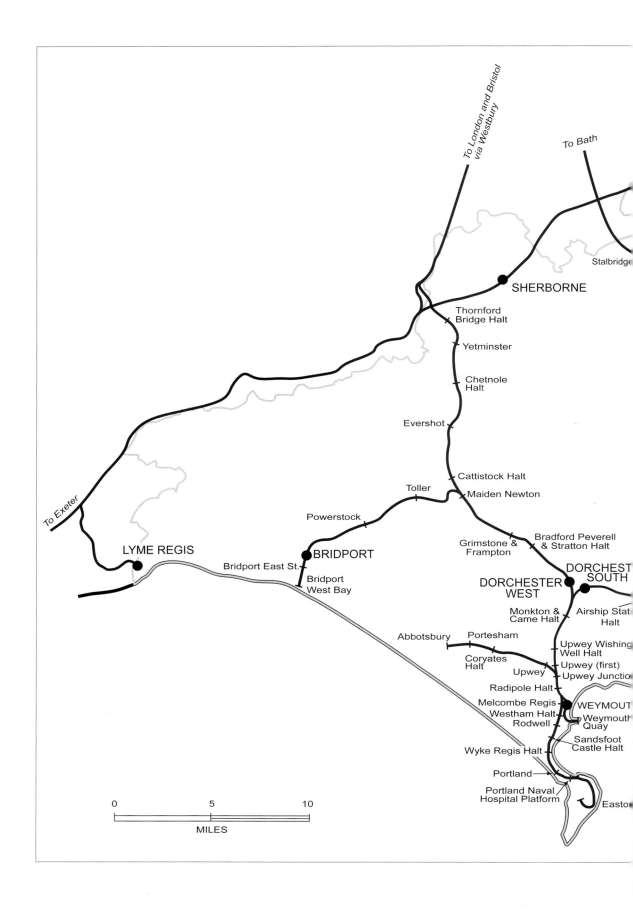

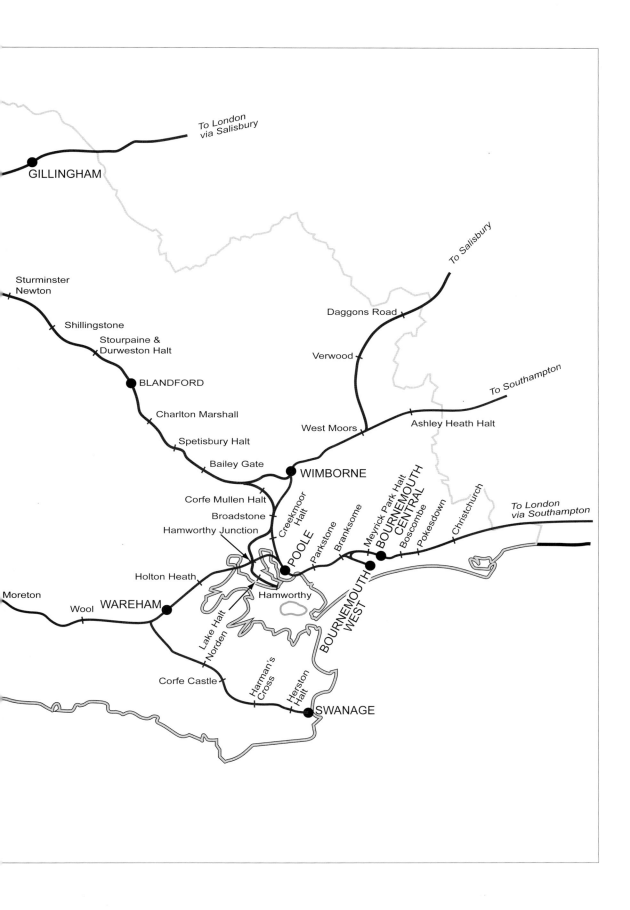

To London
via Salisbury

GILLINGHAM

To Salisbury

Sturminster
Newton

Daggons Road

Shillingstone

Stourpaine &
Durweston Halt

Verwood

To Southampton

BLANDFORD

Charlton Marshall

West Moors

Ashley Heath Halt

Spetisbury Halt

Bailey Gate

WIMBORNE

Corfe Mullen Halt

Creekmoor Halt

Meyrick Park Halt

BOURNEMOUTH
CENTRAL

To London
via Southampton

Broadstone

Parkstone

Branksome

Boscombe

Pokesdown

Christchurch

Hamworthy Junction

POOLE

Holton Heath

Hamworthy

BOURNEMOUTH
WEST

Moreton

Wool

WAREHAM

Lake Halt

Norden

Corfe Castle

Harman's Cross

Herston Halt

SWANAGE

THE STATIONS AND HALTS
THEN & NOW

Dorset's railway stations and halts developed over the years on the expanding network to serve the changing economy and settlements. Facilities were provided to meet the requirements of the towns and villages including long platforms for excursion trains arriving at the coastal resorts, cattle pens for livestock travelling to or from the local markets and various size goods sheds for the storage of products imported for the local community or for export from local industries. Many of the station buildings themselves and the associated buildings including goods sheds, signal boxes and station master's houses were impressive structures reflecting the importance of the railway to the local economy. Often constructed of local materials in the style of the railway company, many were, and some still are, of architectural merit.

Unfortunately many of these buildings have been demolished and a few lie derelict but others remain still in railway use or have been renovated for new uses such as houses or warehouses. A number of sites formerly occupied by the station itself and associated goods yards today have considerable value for redevelopment located close to, or at the heart of, settlements now much expanded compared with their size during the era of railway development in the 19th century. A number of these sites include former railway buildings but in many cases the site has been redeveloped with few or no remnants. A wide variety of uses has taken over these valuable sites for example: industrial/commercial units; housing; new roads or retail units.

On a more positive note, a feature in Dorset, as in many parts of the South West, is the continuing residential use of a number of former station master's houses with the architectural style of the appropriate railway company and nearby station building. In some cases they stand in isolation close to the former station buildings and now may not be in residential use. In some cases they survive standing out in their different building style within a new housing development built on the former site of the station

A good example of the changing use of Dorset's station buildings is Dorchester West. The photograph above shows the station entrance gas lit and still in use in 1968, the one below as a 'Dominos' pizza outlet in October 2015. The building is listed, and the architect Ritson design included a hipped roof, deep eaves and round headed windows.

and goods yard. The former role of the house is often revealed by the name 'Station House' but at others a non-railway related name (eg Rose Villa) is displayed perhaps with the aim of deterring snap happy railway fanatics!

Photographs providing examples of the past and current use of the railway buildings and sites across Dorset follow. Details regarding each station are then set out in the chapter on 'Dorset Stations and Halts 1847-2016'.

ABBOTSBURY

Above: The Station Master, staff and passengers on the platform in the early 1900s.

Above: Looking east from the platform in 1939 towards the Goods Shed which survives today.

Right: The former Goods Shed on 11th March 2016, the only significant remaining building, a new bungalow having been built on the site of the station itself following demolition in January 1963.

ASHLEY HEATH HALT

Above: A train at the down platform heading south towards Wimborne in 1963.

Below: A surviving section of the platform on 10th March 2016. The sign is one of a series on the Castleman Trailway. The insert shows a sign on the Castleman Trailway just to the north of Ashley Heath Halt where the Trailway crosses the road between Three Legged Cross and Ashley.

BAILEY GATE

Top: Looking south east in about 1900.

Above: Looking north west on 7th July 1962, the goods yard on the right.

Right: On 10th March 2016 the entrance to the Bailie Gate industrial estate developed on the site of the station and adjacent dairy. The gatehouse (right) is on the site of the former up platform. Note the spelling 'Bailie'.

BLANDFORD

A 4-4-0 and train arriving at the station in this early view looking south, the goods shed in the left foreground.

A later view looking north on 7th July 1962, the goods yard to the right.

BLANDFORD

Above left: The former station site on 14th February 2016 principally occupied by a car park and surrounded by housing (Station Court). In the distance is the white former station master's house and in the foreground is a locomotive wheel beside a remaining short section of track.

Above right: A close up of the station master's house, to the left is the surviving footbridge not associated directly with the railway connecting Alexander and Oakfield Streets.

Below: Beneath the footbridge a short section of track and buffer stops at the south end of the North Dorset Trailway on 14th February 2016.

BOSCOMBE

Above: A view west on 24th August 1963. Note the covered footbridge and the glazed wind shields at the end of the canopies. The goods yard was located to the left.

Below left: Looking east at the former station site on 22nd October 2015, industrial development on the left and a car wash/valeting depot to the right.

Below right A close up also on 22nd October 2015 of the entrance to the former goods yard once in use as a coal depot now the King's Park Hand Car Wash and Valeting depot.

Above: The building was constructed to give the impression of a glass roofed winter garden, as is illustrated in this interior view of 1911.

Below: Looking east on 22nd October 2015 at the fine building renovated after the serious damage incurred in the 1990 gale.

BOURNEMOUTH CENTRAL (continued)

An early 20th century view of the fine exterior of the down side. Note the cover for passengers arriving and leaving the station.

This view on 22nd October 2015 of the down exterior illustrates the continuing fine features of the station. A bus station on the left now provides good facilities for public transport.

BOURNEMOUTH WEST

Above: An view in about 1910 of the fine exterior, the building sited parallel to the tracks rather than behind the buffers as normally the case at terminus stations.

Left: From a similar viewpoint on 22nd October 2015 the former station site is now the Queens Road Coach and Car Park and a section of the Wessex Way (behind the trees).

Below: Looking down the long platforms on 3rd July 1961. The top of the Midland Hotel can be seen above the middle canopy, this building is now (2016) the Midland Heights apartments.

BRANKSOME

Above: A view west in the 1960s before the canopies were shortened in 1987.

Left: Looking west on 22nd November 2015, the canopies now shortened with only three stanchions. The entrance/booking hall is seen above the up side canopy (right).

Below left: The booking hall in 1961; the sign states 'Southern Railway' 13 years after the company ceased.

Below: The former booking hall on 22nd October 2015 now unused. A previous visit in 2000 recorded the building as the 'Red Lodge' occupied by 'Flagship Quality Flowers'.

BRIDPORT

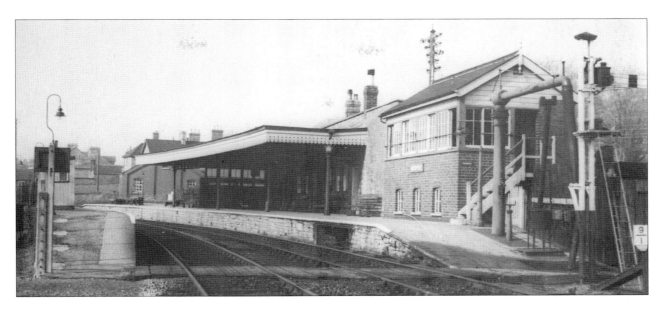

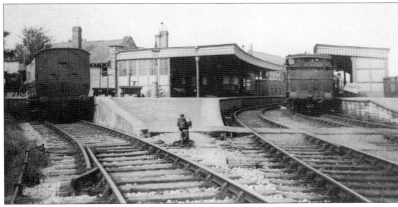

A view from the north on 27th April 1963 showing the virtually unaltered 1857 main building (canopy added mid 1890s), the 1952 down platform metal shelter and the signal box.

In the 1920s a train stands at the down platform on which is the 1890s shelter replaced in 1952 (see above). A carriage is in the short dock siding (left).

Below: The station exterior in the early 1960s.

Below right The station site on 11th March 2016 occupied by a supermarket, a builders merchant (distant) and a section of St Andrews Road realigned along the former line south to Bridport West Bay (foreground).

BRIDPORT EAST STREET

Top: The original station building, a thatched cottage on land purchased for the railway construction and adapted for use as a booking office, waiting room and station master's house. It survived until 1904.

Above left: The second station in 1905 a year after rebuilding, including a station master's house (left) and a building on the platform. A train from West Bay is arriving.

Above: The station building in use as a house in June 1958.

Left: Looking north on 11th March 2016 at the former site of East Street station from Sea Road, a section of the Bridport relief road.

BRIDPORT WEST BAY

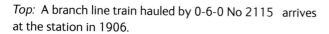

Top: A branch line train hauled by 0-6-0 No 2115 arrives at the station in 1906.

Above: The station site in use as a boat yard in May 1975, the building acting as the office.

Above right: The station building in its role as the West Bay Visitor Centre photographed by the author in May 1999, two carriages standing beside the former platform.

Right: On the 11th March 2016 the 'Station Kitchen' occupying the former station building supplied coffee and cake for the author and his wife.

BROADSTONE

The station exterior in May 1940 incorporating the newsagent, W H Smith.

Above: Looking north on 22nd September 1963, a covered footbridge connects the four long platforms. The Railway Hotel is seen on the far right.

Below left: Another view north showing the station (left) and the impressive Railway Hotel (right), in 2016 renamed 'The Goods Shed' Free House.

Below right From a similar viewpoint on 10th March 2016, the Broadstone Leisure Centre, developed on the former station site (left) and the former Railway Hotel (now The Goods Shed Free House) to the right.

CHARLTON MARSHALL HALT

Looking north on 24th April 1965 nearly nine years after closure for regular passenger services.

A similar view some 50 years later on 10th March 2016, the Stour Valley Way following the former track bed between the surviving platforms.

CHETNOLE HALT

The two wooden short timber platforms on 7th July 1962 on both sides of a road bridge carrying a road to the village a half mile to the east.

On 27th January 2016 a view north from the road bridge of the now concrete platform and shelter on the single track line.

An early view from the road bridge east of the station of two trains in the 1886 station.

Looking west from the same viewpoint on 22nd October 2015.

CHRISTCHURCH

Staff pose outside the 1886 station building early in the 20th century. Note the large roof over the footbridge (left).

The station building exterior on the down (towards Bournemouth) side on 22nd October 2015 relatively little altered compared with the earlier view except the footbridge is now uncovered.

CORFE CASTLE

A view north of the station in the early 1960s showing the main building on the up platform, the shelter on the down and the goods shed (left). The signal box on the down platform beyond the shelter had been demolished in 1956.

A similar view north on 13th December 2015 from the new footbridge of the renovated building and shelter and the reconstructed signal box.

Looking south east across the station in the 1960s. The board crossings were the only means of walking between platforms.

CORFE CASTLE

Above: A 1963 view of the south facade. From left to right: the gents, the ladies room, the booking hall and the large station master's house.

Right: The virtually unaltered south façade on 13th December 2015.

Lower right: The restored goods shed in use as a museum on the 13th December 2015.

DAGGONS ROAD

Top: An Adams 460 class 4-4-0 arrives at the single platform station with a down (towards Wimborne) train.

Above: Looking down on the station from the road bridge south of the station on 2nd May 1964 showing from left to right the station master's house, the booking office and the ladies room. There was no platform canopy.

Left: Looking down the former station approach road on 10th March 2016. From right to left: the former station master's house 'The Old Station Cottage' and three new houses 'The Old Waiting Room', 'The Sidings' and 'Buffers'.

DORCHESTER SOUTH

The original up (right) and short down (centre) platforms and the 1879 curved down platform and shelter (left). The timber built train shed (centre) covers the straight tracks and the short down platform.

The 1879 curved down platform and shelter (right) and the 1970 up platform (left) in June 1984.

The up platform with the booking office and shelter seen through the new footbridge on 30th October 2015.

A new curved up (towards Wareham) platform came into use on 28th June 1970 but the old building continued to be used for 17 years. This elevated walkway connected the building and platform.

Below: The exterior building behind the up platform in June 1984.

Below: The entrance to the station on 30th October 2015 including the booking office (centre) which came into use in November 1987.

Below: The down side brick and metal shelter which replaced the 1879 shelter in 1987, photographed on 30th October 2015.

DORCHESTER WEST

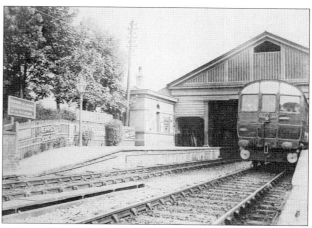

Above: A view north in about 1930 of the timber train shed which covered both platforms and the double tracks from the early days. It was demolished in 1934.

Above: A rail motor stands at the north end of the train shed.

Looking north from the Weymouth Avenue road bridge in the 1950s. The former broad gauge goods shed is on the right.

Looking north from the same viewpoint on 30th October 2015. Industrial and retail units have replaced the goods shed and yard. Housing has developed above the line to the left.

A view north in about 1950 showing the fine canopies that replaced the train shed in 1934.

From the same viewpoint on the 30th October 2015, a metal and glass shelter has replaced the building on the up (towards Yeovil) platform. The 1047 hrs train to Weymouth is at the down platform.

EASTON

Above: A view north in about 1912, four staff pose for the camera and a lady with her dog sits on the seat.

Right: The Ladymead elderly persons housing development which now occupies much of the station site on 10th November 2015.

Below: The damaged station following a fire on the 28th November 1903. It was rebuilt in its original form in 1904.

Below: The station forecourt in about 1950, note the narrow canopy over the entrance.

GILLINGHAM

Left: A fine view early in the 20th century of a Yeovil bound train and the impressive William Tite designed building on the up platform. Note the nameboard, 'Gillingham for Mere'.

Below: The up side building on 24th November 2015 is virtually unaltered from the earlier photograph.

Below: Looking down from the 1967 concrete footbridge at the little altered up side building on 24th November 2015. A metal and glass shelter serves passengers on the down platform replacing the previous brick building.

Below left: The exterior in October 1981.

Below: The scene outside the station is little changed on 24th November 2015 except for a ticket machine and shelter and the absence of tall chimneys.

HAMWORTHY JUNCTION

The first station, known initially as Poole Junction, sited at the junction between the Southampton and Dorchester Railway and the branch line that ran south to the first Poole station. It was demolished in 1892.

The second 1893 station on 16th March 1963 with the standard 2-6-0 No.76012 standing at the west end of the Hamworthy branch platform.

Below: A view in the 1950s of the 1893 up side building exterior with the station master's house to the left.

Below: The surviving 1893 up side building disused on 30th October 2015. The station master's house has gone.

A close up of the platforms on 15th April 1967, note the wind shield under the canopy on the up platform (left).

A view looking east on the down platform on 30th October 2015, the 1893 down side island platform building was demolished in 1972 now replaced by a 1998 metal and glass shelter. The 1253 hrs train to London (Waterloo) is leaving the up platform.

HOLTON HEATH

Opened originally in April 1916 for workers at the Admiralty Cordite Works and to the public from 1924, this view looking east is dated 16th March 1963.

A train from London (Waterloo) to Weymouth speeds through at about 1345hrs on the 30th October 2015. Metal and glass shelters serve passengers on both platforms replacing the basic canopies seen in the 1963 photo.

A general view looking south east in about 1900 across the station site, the northern extension of the building was initially used as a bookstall and later as a store. The goods shed here at the southern end of the site was later moved to opposite the station building.

A view from a similar point across the former station site on 24th November 2015 showing the commercial units.

LYME REGIS

Top: A train for Axminster departs from the station on 23rd February 1952.

Above: The exterior of the station building on the 27th November 1965, two days prior to its closure for passenger traffic.

Right: Looking north within the former station site on the 24th November 2015 almost exactly 50 years after the station closure , the former building location being near the industrial units on the right.

MAIDEN NEWTON

Above: Looking north in about 1905. The platforms are connected by an open lattice style footbridge. The first signal box stands on the down platform.

Right: From a similar viewpoint on 27th January 2016. The footbridge is now a concrete structure recycled from a closed station on the Salisbury – Exeter line.

Left: The exterior of the station building behind the up platform on 14th April 1968.

Below Left: The exterior 48 years later on 27th January 2016 – little has changed.

Below: The old and new! The boarded up second signal box at the end of the down platform and the metal hut containing the token now necessary for use of the single track section south to Dorchester.

MAIDEN NEWTON

A view south from the northern end of the up (towards Yeovil) platform. To the right is a timber shed over the Bridport branch bay platform and single track. It is adjacent to the north end of the main building. Note the lattice footbridge.

Looking south on 27th January 2016. To the right the train shed and branch line track have gone, the alignment now a footpath. Note the concrete footbridge replacing the original lattice style version.

Within the timber shed over the Bridport branch track. The windows at the far end beyond the buffers are in the northern end wall of the main building.

From the same viewpoint on 27th January 2016 now standing on the footpath. Note the two windows at the end of the building seen in the earlier photo (left).

MELCOMBE REGIS

A view on 3rd February 2016 of the Swannery Court housing complex which occupies part of the former station site.

Looking north on 8th October 1961. Note the large iron screen opposite the platform acting as a wind break in this exposed position overlooking the Backwater.

MORETON

This view on 1st February 1964 shows the main building on the up (towards Wareham) platform, the down side wooden shelter and the signal box beyond the level crossing gates.

Over 50 years later on 13th December 2015 the main building, wooden shelter and signal box have gone, passengers are served by small metal and glass shelters.

PARKSTONE

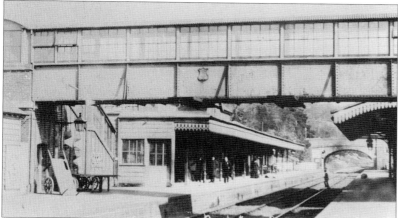

A view east towards Bournemouth on 16th March 1963 shows that the footbridge has lost its roof but the gas lights are still there. Note the wind shields at both ends of the canopy on the up platform behind which the large building incorporates the station master's house.

A view in about 1910 east through the then covered footbridge erected in 1888. The different platform canopy designs indicate varying construction dates.

Looking down from the footbridge on 22nd October 2015. The down side building has gone, passengers served by a metal and glass shelter. The up platform wind shields have also gone.

POKESDOWN

The original 1886 station building and signal box on the long island platform.

Reconstruction work in progress in 1931, the original island platform (centre) being replaced by two long side platforms between which 4 tracks were laid.

Left: A general view east of the station on 22nd October 2015, basically unchanged from the 1931 reconstruction except the two central tracks have gone.

Below Left: The station entrance in the 1930s with the sign 'Southern Railway'.

Below: The entrance on the 22nd October 2015, the sign stating 'Pokesdown for Boscombe'.

POOLE

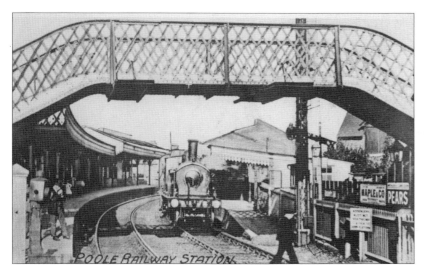

A S&D 4-4-0 at the head of a **Somerset and Dorset Railway** train on route to Bournemouth West in about 1910. These structures sited on a sharp curve and incorporating a mixture of canopy designs were demolished in 1969 when the Towngate bridge was constructed over the site.

Below: A view east on 24th August 1963 some 6 years before these buildings were demolished. A train is departing from the up platform towards Bournemouth.

Below: The 'clasp' style buildings, that served passengers from 1969 until 1988, on 31st May 1977.

Right: Looking down from the footbridge on 22nd October 2015 at the 1988 station building, the vaulted roof suspended from four columns.

PORTESHAM

Top: Looking west towards Abbotsbury, the goods shed is on the right opposite the single platform.

Above: A view to the east in 1947. Access to the platform was via the white gate adjacent to the building.

Left: The former station building on 11th March 2016, now 'Sleepers' available for holiday letting. All three chimneys still survive.

PORTLAND

An old postcard of the 'Royal Hotel & Railway Station, Portland' illustrates the location of the first station (left) at the northern end of Victoria Square.

A comparable view on 3rd February 2016 with the Royal Victoria Hotel (unfortunately boarded up) and a roundabout in the distance partially covering the site of the first station.

A horse drawn carriage stands in front of the first station in Victoria Square in April 1904.

A close up of the first passenger station in use as a goods station on 6th February 1965.

The second station on the extension to Easton viewed in the Weymouth direction, under construction in 1905.

The staff at the second station in 1909. Note the early timber framework of the down platform (right), the station being constructed on land reclaimed from the Portland Harbour foreshore. The platforms were later reconstructed with stone and concrete components.

POWERSTOCK

Looking west on the 27th April 1963 to the right is the site of the former goods yard which closed in 1961. The building has been in residential use since 1970 some 5 years before the station closed to passenger traffic.

The rear of the station building with a very short platform overlooking the goods yard.

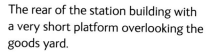

The entrance to the former station on 27th January 2016. The building, in residential use, is in the middle distance. The sign by the gate states 'The Old Station'.

RADIPOLE HALT

Looking north at the halt used by the author in his young days. Note the pagoda style shelters and the path to the down platform from a gate adjacent to the Spa Road bridge.

The deserted site on 3rd February 2016, the line of the footpath to the down platform is clearly visible.

RODWELL

Left: Staff and passengers pose for the photographer on the single platform in 1906 before the second platform opened.

Below: A rare early view of the 1907 up platform with the pagoda hut and second signal box. The lattice footbridge was added that year.

Below right: A view north in 1945 showing the concrete hut on the down platform replacing the building destroyed by bombing in 1941.

Above: The same viewpoint on 10th November 2015, the former track bed now a section of the Rodwell Trail from Weymouth to Wyke Regis.

SANDSFOOT CASTLE

Above: Passengers at the halt on 1st March 1952, the last day of passenger services.

Right: The surviving platforms on 6th February 1965, almost 13 years after the halt's closure.

Below right A small surviving section of the wooden platform beside the Rodwell Trail with a Trail sign on 10th November 2015.

SHERBORNE

Top: A rare but poor quality image of the early facilities prior to the installation of a footbridge in 1886 shows the William Tite building on the up (towards Gillingham) platform (including accommodation for the station master) and a small shelter on the down.

Above: A busy scene on the up platform in the 1930s, including the 1886 unglazed covered footbridge and an arched canopy on the down platform erected in 1926. On the up platform is a W H Smith bookstall.

Right: A plaque on a wall of the up side building commemorating the 150th anniversary of the station's opening in May 1860.

Salisbury & Yeovil Railway Company
To commemorate
the 150th anniversary of the
opening of Sherborne Railway Station
on 7 May 1860
this plaque was unveiled by Paul Atterbury
railway writer and broadcaster
on 8 May 2010
Network Rail & South West Trains

SHERBORNE

Another view east on 10th May 1964, the canopy is a recent 1962 structure replacing the 1926 arched canopy.

The view east on 28th January 2016, the facilities similar to those in 1964 with the addition of a new extension to the building on the up side which incorporates the gents toilets.

The exterior on 28th January 2016. The principal change from 1967 is the rebuilt structure at the southern end of the building incorporating the gents toilets.

The station exterior in 1967.

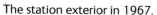

SHILLINGSTONE

Looking north on 7th July 1962 showing the main building with its ornate canopy on the up platform and a shelter on the down.

Left: The main building and former parcels office survive in a semi derelict state on 5th April 1999.

Below left: A close up of the renovated building incorporating a shop and tea room, the restored carriage acting as a overflow facility for the tea room. Note the fine restored canopy.

Below: A view north on the 14th February 2016 of the renovated main building on the up platform and a replacement shelter in the course of construction on the down.

SPETISBURY

A down (towards Poole) train approaches before the doubling of the line in 1901. The buildings shown were replaced by a shelter when new larger structures were erected on the new up platform.

Staff on the platform and the station building erected on the new up platform following doubling of the line in 1901.

Below: The surviving platforms on 24th April 1965 and, some 50 years later on 10th March 2016, the former facilities undergoing renovation by the 'Spetisbury Station Project'.

STALBRIDGE

Looking north from the level crossing gates on Station Road on 7th July 1962 showing from left to right the signal box, the booking office and the station master's house on the up platform. A small shelter stands on the down platform.

The station buildings and signal box with the level crossing gates in place for rail use.

The station site on 14th February 2016 occupied by a large industrial unit. In the foreground is a section of a former extension of the track through the goods yard serving a Ministry of Food depot during the Second World War. Off right is a hump on Station Road indicating the former location of the level crossing.

STURMINSTER NEWTON

A general view north west of the station on 7th July 1962 including the wooden signal box at the end of the up platform and a small wooden shelter with a fretted canopy on the down.

A detailed view of the main building on the up platform and the goods shed at the end of the down. Note the dip in the platform edge of the up platform leading to the board crossing to the end of the down.

Left: The site of the station on 16th February 2016 now occupied by the road and car parking. The commemorative gateway to the Railway Gardens can be seen behind the right hand tree in the centre of the photo.

Below left: The commemorative gateway erected in 2007 at the entrance to the now named 'Railway Gardens' originally laid out in 1992 on the infilled cutting north of the closed station.

Below right On 16th February 2016 a close up of the plaque that can be seen on the pillar to the left of the gates.

SWANAGE

Staff pose on the platform probably in 1887 beside engine 2-4-0 no. 209 at the head of a train to Wareham. The building was extensively rebuilt and extended at the east end in 1937/38, the station master's house behind the nameboard being retained almost unaltered.

A general view looking east of the station site on 7th July 1963 showing from left to right a through train (ie beyond Wareham) in the main platform, a local train in the bay platform, the large goods shed, the signal box and carriages in a siding alongside coaches parked in front of the building.

The restored Swanage station from Gilbert Road, a busy scene on 13th December 2015 with the operation of 'Santa Specials'.

SWANAGE

Left: Looking west in the 1960s from the buffers at the main platform, the run round loop line and a spare carriage.

Below: From the east a view of the 1938 Purbeck stone building which blended well with the 1885 original station master's house. Of interest is the Benn and Cronin indicator (centre) which for many years displayed the train departure times.

The front façade of the station in its British Railways days; to the left is the 1885 station master's house whilst the remainder of the building largely dates from the major 1937/8 development.

The façade of the 1937/8 building on 13th December 2015. The two bus shelters reflect the sign above the entrance 'Swanage Travel Interchange'.

The large goods shed, extended in 1898 and 1937, used today by the Swanage Railway for carriage restoration and maintenance.

A plaque on the east end of the station building.

THORNFORD BRIDGE HALT

A view on 7th July 1962 of the staggered timber platforms either side of the road bridge about a mile south west of Thornford village.

Looking down from the road bridge on 27th January 2016 at the one remaining platform and hut, concrete components recycled from Cattistock Halt following its closure in 1966.

TOLLER

Looking north east at the station on 27th April 1963. Six years after its closure in 1975 the station building was dismantled and re-assembled on the platform at Totnes Littlehempston on the South Devon Railway.

Much of the platform survives and in this photo of 27th January 2016 the west end is a section of a footpath.

UPWEY (on Abbotsbury Branch)

Top: The station looking west from the Dorchester Road bridge. Note the large goods shed.

Above: Looking west from the same viewpoint on 3rd February 2016, the site largely used by a builders merchant 'Buildrite'. The surviving station building can be seen in the centre behind the shelves of wood.

Left: The former goods shed in commercial use on 3rd February 2016.

Above: Looking north towards Dorchester in the 1930s, the main building and corrugated iron hut on the up platform and a shelter with a narrow fretted canopy on the down. The main building serves passengers on the main line platform and the Abbotsbury branch platform behind the fence (left).

Left: From a similar viewpoint looking north on 3rd February 2016, passengers using the main line now served by metal and glass shelters. The footbridge survives. To the left cars are in a car park developed on the track bed of the former branch line.

From a similar viewpoint to the photograph on the left, taken on 3rd February 2016. The raised stone areas are remains of the lower sections of the former main building demolished in 1972. The road and car park were laid in 1986 along the former branch trackbed.

A view north along the branch platform in the 1930s, the track falling sharply towards Upwey station and Abbotsbury. The narrow high canopy offers scant shelter for passengers.

VERWOOD

Above: A view looking north at Verwood station in the 1950s, the main building, signal box and parcels office on the up platform (towards Salisbury). The roof of the Albion Hotel sited in the station yard can be seen over the main building and signal box.

Right: The only surviving reminder of the railway at Verwood on 10th March 2016. The road over bridge became redundant when the B3081 was realigned south of the Albion Hotel whose conservatory is seen on the left.

The rear of the station can be seen just to the left of the telegraph pole. The Albion Hotel (left) overlooks the station yard. At this time the B3081 is aligned to the north of the Hotel (off to the left over the bridge).

From a similar viewpoint on 10th March 2016. The road is on its revised alignment south of the Hotel, the station being originally sited close to the passing car.

A rare view west of the first station east of the level crossing.

Below: A general view on 11th May 1985 looking west from the east end of the up platform. The Swanage branch platform is at the far end of the down platform (left).

Above: From a similar viewpoint looking west on 30th October 2015, the scene is very little changed from 1985.

Below: The building is very little changed in this photo of 30th October 2015.

Below: The exterior of the 1886 main building on the down side on 29th March 1987.

WESTHAM HALT

Right: A goods train from Portland passes over the Littlefield level crossing in 1951. Weymouth Grammar School children stand by the ticket hut at the entrance to the halt. The platform shelter can just be seen above the hut.

Below: A goods train has just passed through the halt on 11th February 1965. To the right is the signal box within which a wheel operated the level crossing gates.

Lower right: A view from a similar point on 10th November 2015, the track bed used here at the northern end of the Rodwell Trail.

Lower left: At the end of the surviving platform is a sign 'Westham Halt' erected in association with the Trail.

WEST MOORS

A goods train passes through the station in August 1958, the principal building is on the up (towards Ringwood) platform. A wooden shelter stands on the down. The unusual concrete footbridge was erected during the 1900s.

Below left: Looking north east on 10th March 2016 along the alignment of the original Southampton and Dorchester Railway 'Castleman's Corkscrew', hence the names of the Trail that now uses the track bed and the elderly persons housing (left) that now occupies the site of the station.

Below right The 'Tap and Railway' public house on 10th March 2016 to the south west of the B3072 opposite the station site, the original name being the 'Railway Hotel'.

WEYMOUTH

Above: A fine comprehensive view from the signal box in September 1931 showing the central roof covering the main platforms and train sheds over the side platforms. Both Southern and Great Western locomotives are operating though, by this time, the GWR was responsible for the whole complex.

Above: The original 1850s overall roof seen from the junction of King Street and Queen Street in about 1913. The tracks extended beyond the roof to buffers close behind the fence permitting locomotives to discharge smoke and steam in the open air.

From the same viewpoint on 3rd February 2016, the Somerset Hotel remains the same (right) but the distant view has completely changed with the 1986 rebuilt station fronted by a car park and access road.

WEYMOUTH (continued)

The exterior of the up (western) side of the timber first station building on 7th August 1981, some 5 years before its demolition.

Left: The 1986 second building from across the car park on 3rd February 2016.

Below: Looking back along the three operating platforms of the 1986 station on 3rd February 2016, that to the right used by GWR trains to Bristol and beyond and the central island platform by South West trains to London (Waterloo).

WEYMOUTH QUAY

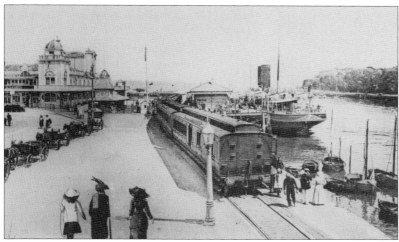

Above: A train at the 1889 Quay station during the first decade of the 20th century prior to the construction of the first Pavilion Theatre left of the station which opened in 1908.

Left: A later view of a long train at the station following the completion and opening of the first Pavilion Theatre in 1908.

Below: The 1972 Quay building unused when photographed on 3rd February 2016. The boat trains stopped using the station in September 1987 but the building continued to be used by passengers on the ferry services to the Channel Islands, which have also now ceased.

The 1933 station building on 20th January 1962. This was replaced in 1972.

WIMBORNE

Above: Looking north towards Ringwood on 29th May 1966 along the curved platforms.

Right: From the north end of the station in 1963, note the unusually tall signal box designed to assist visibility through the station site.

Below: A plaque on the wall of one of the units photographed on 10th March 2016 close to the entrance into the Business Park (below)..

Above: The exterior of the station building, its appearance not enhanced by the flat roofed extensions.

Left: Units in the Riverside Business Park which now occupies part of the former station site.

WOOL

Right: Looking east from the footbridge on 4th June 1967, the unusually long upside shelter serves passengers on the up platform.

Below: A view east towards the level crossing in 1969 showing the main building on the down line, a long wooden shelter on the up (towards Wareham) and a lattice style open footbridge.

Below: From the footbridge nearly 50 years later on 13th December 2015. The main building had been replaced in 1969 by this featureless prefabricated building, the long shelter by a metal and glass shelter.

Below: The down 1969 building on 13th December 2015.

WYKE REGIS

The Halt in 1909 and a GWR steam railmotor and trailer on a single track section of the Weymouth to Portland line.

A LSWR C14 class 2-2-0T No. 742 hauling a motor train set on route to Portland approaching the Halt in about 1910.

Below: Remains of the Halt survive. In this photo, taken on 10th November 2015, they are buried in undergrowth to the left of the author's rucksack lying beside the Rodwell Trail which follows the track bed of the former Weymouth/Portland line from Westham to Wyke.

The exact site was identified by a glimpse of the Rodwell Trail sign.

YETMINSTER

Above: A view looking north in about 1962 of the main building on the up (towards Yeovil) platform. A stone waiting shelter stands on the down behind which is the station master's house.

Right: The station is now a request stop for services between Weymouth and Yeovil. On the 27th January 2016 the 1110hrs train from Weymouth to Gloucester passes through the station non-stop.

Below: The station house behind the former down (towards Dorchester) platform on 3rd February 2016.

A plaque attached to the southern wall of the building to the left of the train.

HUNDRED OF YETMINSTER HISTORY SOCIETY
YETMINSTER STATION
150th ANNIVERSARY
of the
FIRST PASSENGER SERVICE
20th January 1857
2007

DORSET STATIONS AND HALTS 1847 – 2016

SCHEDULE SHOWING GRID REFERENCE, OPENING AND CLOSING DATES
AND RECENT/CURRENT USE OF THE BUILDINGS AND SITES

ABBOTSBURY SY 582853

Opened: 9th November 1885 (with the opening of the Abbotsbury Railway).

Closed: Passengers and Goods – 1st December 1952 (with closure of the Abbotsbury branch).

A classic example of a GWR branch line terminus, the station opened in 1885 about a quarter of a mile east of the village. The main yellow stone station building, standing on the south side of the line, was designed, as others on the branch, by William Clarke. Oil lit throughout its history, it incorporated a ladies' room and toilets, gentlemen's toilets and a general waiting room through which was access to a booking hall. Features of the building included its distinctive roof of blue and red tiles alternating every third row and three tall chimneys; the 275 ft. long platform was covered in front of the building by a large canopy with a fretted valence; by the 1930s its depth had been reduced. For a few years before the Second World War a GWR camping coach stood on a short siding behind the east end of the platform. Cattle pens and a goods shed stood on the south side of the line at the east end of the station.

In 1904 the Prince and Princess of Wales passed through the station when paying a visit to the Fleet; 44 years later the station was the location for filming 'The Small Back Room'. For many years Abbotsbury was a destination for Sunday School trips from the Weymouth area, the nearby fields providing good facilities for games and picnics. The station buildings were demolished in January 1963; by 1970 the site was occupied by a bungalow, the garage standing on the site of the station building. The platform survives with the edge intact though difficult to see in undergrowth. Many of the stones from the demolished building were re-used in building a wall around the garden. The former station approach road from the Abbotsbury to Portesham road now leads towards the bungalow and a public footpath follows the former track bed through the

station site. The former goods shed remains alongside the footpath.

AIRSHIP STATION HALT SY 765891

Opened: 1919 (on the Wareham – Dorchester line originally opened in 1847)

Closed: c.1923

A short lived halt to the west of Moreton station which served the nearby Airship station which opened in 1918.

ASHLEY HEATH HALT SU 114047

Opened: 1st April 1927 (on the Southampton to Dorchester Railway originally opened in 1847).

Closed: 4th May 1964 (with closure of the Ringwood – Broadstone line to passenger traffic).

The halt opened in April 1927 some 80 years after services on the Southampton and Dorchester Railway (Castleman's Corkscrew) commenced through the site. Sited to the west of what was known as Woolsbridge Crossing, the aim was to serve the growing residential areas west of Ringwood, Ashley, St Ives and St Leonards. The halt comprised two concrete platforms, each with a shelter, and a siding for goods traffic behind the down (south) platform. Following closure in 1964, the former track bed is now a section of the Castleman Trailway; the former down platform has gone but a section of the up platform remains together with the name board and a Trailway information board, having been restored by local residents. The information board states that "The restored halt is a fitting memorial to local resident Brian Kliger who died in 2011. Brian was a volunteer station master with Swanage Railway and an active conservation volunteer at Avon Heath and Lions Hill".

BAILEY GATE   SY 949994

Opened: 1st November 1860 (with the opening of the Wimborne – Blandford St Mary section of the Dorset Central Railway). *Sturminster Marshall until 31st August 1863 then renamed Bailey Gate to avoid confusion with Sturminster Newton.*

Closed: Passengers – 7th March 1966 (with closure of the Somerset and Dorset Railway, Bath Green Park to Poole, to passenger traffic). Goods – 5th April 1965 (milk traffic continued to be transported until 1969 when the line closed).

Named Bailey Gate in 1863, to avoid confusion between its initial name of Sturminster Marshall and the newly opened Sturminster Newton station, its principal role was indicated in the station name board 'Bailey Gate for Sturminster Marshall'. The station served not only the residents of the adjacent Sturminster Marshall but also handled considerable freight traffic generated by the nearby United Dairies milk processing factory. The goods yard north of the station expanded over the years with extensive sidings to cope with this traffic. The station buildings, of a basic Dorset Central Railway design, included a brick building, incorporating the main facilities, and a wooden porters' cabin on the down platform and a small wooden shelter on the up. The platforms were linked by a timber board crossing at the northern end. The platforms remained in situ for some twenty years after the station closed for passenger traffic in March 1966; the track was lifted through the station on 21st June 1970. The station buildings were demolished by 1973; the signal box was demolished just before the track was lifted. Following complete clearance in April 1992, the former station site, goods yard and dairy were redeveloped as the Baillie Gate (note different spelling) industrial estate with new units and an entrance gatehouse built on the site of the up platform.

BLANDFORD   ST 888066

Opened: Temporary station opened at Blandford St Mary 1st November 1860 (at the northern end of the Dorset Central Railway from Wimborne). Closed and replaced by the permanent Blandford station 10th September 1863 (with the commencement of services on the Blandford St Mary – Blandford – Templecombe section of the Somerset and Dorset Railway – formal opening 31st August 1863). *The suffix 'Forum' was added to the station name from 21st September 1953.*

Closed: Passengers – 7th March 1966 (with closure of the Somerset and Dorset Railway, Bath Green Park - Poole to

passenger traffic). Goods – 13th February 1967 (some 'carted by public' traffic continued until final closure on 6th January 1969).

Located close to the town centre, the 1863 station played a significant role in developing and enhancing Blandford's status in the Victorian era, a typical feature of many towns both in Dorset and throughout the country. A further typical feature was the traffic generated by local schools, in this case from 1927, Bryanston School (hence the station name board 'Blandford Forum for Bryanston School') and also Blandford Grammar School. The nearby military camps also generated significant traffic at Blandford station particularly during the two World Wars.

The station buildings, of Dorset Central Railway design, were not only the largest but considered by many as the most impressive on the Somerset and Dorset Railway (apart from Bath Green Park that is!). The principal building on the up platform was brick built with stone facing and a large canopy. During the Second World War a canteen stood on this platform serving the troops. The smaller shelter on the slightly shorter down platform was dominated by a tall 27 lever signal box erected in 1893 which replaced an earlier box on the up platform. This second signal box was rebuilt in 1906 following a fire started by lightning in a thunderstorm on the 23rd June of the same year. The platforms were connected by a subway. The footbridge to the north of the station was a public facility not associated with the railway connecting Alexander and Oakfield Streets. Adjacent to the footbridge was the station master's house in front of which was the goods yard incorporating a large goods shed and cattle pens.

The whole site is now redeveloped as housing (Station Court) following clearance in August 1973; much of the former goods yard is a car park (Station Court Car Park), a short section of track originally in a goods yard siding survives across the entrance. Another short section of track with a buffer stop is laid almost beneath the footbridge at the southern end of the North Dorset Trailway which follows the former track bed to Sturminster Newton. Alongside is the former station master's house continuing in residential use with the name 'Station House'. Completing the railway theme, a locomotive wheel has also been installed beside a further short section of track just inside the car park.

BOSCOMBE   SZ 114924

Opened: 1st June 1897 (on the Christchurch – Bournemouth line originally opened in 1870).

Closed: Passengers – 4th October 1965. Goods – 1st May 1972.

Opened following a long campaign by local residents, the facilities comprised two long side platforms on which stood large shelters with ornate canopies and glazed platform wind breaks. The main building on the up side was surmounted by tall chimneys. Overall the station buildings were of a style being used by the London and South Western Railway in the 1890s. Following complete closure in the early 1970s, the buildings were demolished; the site has since been in various uses including the Bournemouth Car Centre in the late 1990s and a coal depot on the former goods yard on the down side. When visited in October 2015 the down side was occupied by 'Kings Park Hand Car Wash' and on the up side was industrial development.

BOURNEMOUTH CENTRAL   SZ 097920

Opened: First station opened as 'Bournemouth' 18th March 1870 as the terminus of the Christchurch – Bournemouth extension of the Ringwood – Christchurch line opened in 1862. (*suffix 'East' added in 1874 with the opening of Bournemouth West station*). Second station opened 20th July 1885 (*suffix changed to 'Central' 1st July 1893 and remained until 10th July 1967*).
Closed: Passengers – remains open for services on the London Waterloo – Weymouth line. Goods – 2nd July 1979.

The first station, sited close to the centre of the growing resort, was a small terminus station at the end of the 1870 single line extension from Christchurch of the Ringwood to Christchurch line. Sited to the east of Holdenhurst Road, opposite the site of the current station, there was only a single platform with minimum shelter. With demands for improved facilities and the opening of the line from this first station west across the town towards Poole and the 1874 Bournemouth West station, a major new building opened in 1885 west of Holdenhurst Road, the original station being then used for some years for goods traffic only. Built in a style to give the impression of a glass roofed winter garden to accord with the need to meet the needs of the expanding tourist trade, impressive facilities were installed and over the years these were enhanced. However the fine details and in particular the high glazed roof brought significant maintenance problems and in the 1980s demolition was even proposed. This was refused, a key factor being its status as a listed building. Problems increased when the 1990 severe gale caused serious damage particularly to the roof and during the 1990s using the station was a depressing experience. Fortunately significant funding became available and a major renovation was completed in 2000, work on the rebuilt

roof alone costing over £6 million. A visit in October 2015 confirmed that Bournemouth Central station remains in excellent condition.

BOURNEMOUTH WEST   SZ 076914

Opened: 15th June 1874 (as the terminus of the LSWR branch line from Poole).
Closed: Passengers and Goods – 4th October 1965 (with closure of the line to Bournemouth West, passenger trains were withdrawn from 6th September).

Opened in 1874 as the terminus of the single track branch line from Poole, the station initially comprised two converted cottages and a single platform; further buildings were added in 1885. In 1888 a significant complex was developed including six platforms with extensive canopies. The principal buildings, unusually for a terminus station, were parallel to the tracks not at right angles; there was no overall roof. Two of the platforms were very long in order to accommodate major trains from London including the 'Bournemouth Belle' which for many years started from this station. Following the electrification of the main line to London serving Bournemouth Central, passenger services to Bournemouth Central ceased in October 1965 and the buildings were demolished in March 1970. Much of the large site was used for the construction of a section of the Wessex Way (A35 by-pass), the remainder as the Queens Road coach and car park. The adjacent former, appropriately named, Midland Hotel building survives as the Midland Heights apartments and flats.

BRADFORD PEVERELL AND STRATTON HALT
SY 657937

Opened: 22nd May 1933 (on the Yeovil – Dorchester line originally opened by the Wilts, Somerset and Weymouth Railway (GWR) in 1857).
Closed: 3rd October 1966.

Serving the villages of Bradford Peverell to the south west and Stratton to the north west, the halt opened in 1933 close to the A37; it initially comprised two wooden 150 long staggered platforms with shelters costing £575. These were replaced in 1959 by concrete platforms and shelters. Closed in 1966, the two concrete platforms survive though much overgrown.

BRANKSOME   SZ 058920

Opened: 1st June 1893 (on the Poole – Bournemouth line originally opened in 1888). Passenger station only.

Closed: remains open for passenger services on the London (Waterloo) – Weymouth line.

A late addition to Bournemouth's rail facilities, this station was originally planned, but not built, as an island platform similar to the first Pokesdown station. The conventional brick built LSWR station comprises two side platforms with long canopies linked by a covered footbridge. The principal building, incorporating the booking hall, is at ground level on the up side. The canopies were cut back in 1987 and the building roof was repaired. When visited in early 2000, the former booking hall, called 'Red Lodge' was occupied by 'Flagship Quality Flowers'; a further visit in October 2015 indicated that the booking hall was no longer in use. The nearby Branksome Railway Hotel provided refreshments for the author!

new down platform with a canopy and a wood/corrugated iron shelter was also provided. In 1952 this canopy, in need of major repairs was demolished and a small metal shelter was installed replacing the 1894 shelter. The original 1857 main station building was incorporated in the reconstruction and remained virtually unaltered until the station's closure in 1975. The antique gas lighting at the station was retained in the 1894 reconstruction and also remained until 1975. To the north west of the station was the goods yard, incorporating a large goods shed close to the station, and cattle pens. A small engine shed stood behind the up platform. All traces of the station complex have been obliterated by the realignment of the main Bridport to Bradpole road, a supermarket and builders merchant.

BRIDPORT SY 475934

Opened: 12th November 1857 (with the opening of the Bridport Railway, Maiden Newton – Bridport). *Known as Bradpole Road 1887 – 1902 but not shown as this in timetable.*
Closed: Passengers – 5th May 1975 (with closure of the Bridport line) Goods – 5th April 1975.
Unstaffed: 6th October 1969.

The opening of the Bridport Railway in 1857 revolutionised life both in the rural areas of west Dorset and in Bridport itself: raw materials for the town's net and twine factories could be imported and the finished products exported more easily. The station became a focus for milk traffic generated by the surrounding rural area, milk being delivered by road in churns and then despatched by rail. Located a mile north of the town centre on the road to Bradpole (a siting considered a drawback), the original stone built terminus costing about £1300 had two platforms under a wooden train shed. The original curved alignment of the station buildings continued throughout their life. The 1884 single track extension to West Bay brought significant changes: one track under the train shed was removed to allow the other to be slewed into a revised curve linking to the extension track, the platform face being rebuilt along the revised alignment. In 1892 the Bridport Railway decided to designate the station, then known as Bradpole Road, as the town's main station. (East Street station was also considered for this role being closer to the town centre.) Following this decision, upgrading of the station commenced in 1894: the train shed was removed and the original platform, now the up platform, was lengthened and a canopy erected. A

BRIDPORT EAST STREET SY 471928

Opened: 31st March 1884 (with the opening of the extension of the Bridport Railway to West Bay). Passenger station only.
Closed: 22nd September 1930 (temporary closure 31st December 1915 – 7th July 1919).

Sited at the eastern end of East Street close to the town centre, the original 1884 station was a nearby thatched cottage on land purchased for railway construction converted into a booking office, waiting room and station master's accommodation. Thus passengers requiring shelter in the very early days had to wait a short distance away from the platform. In response to complaints, a waiting room was erected on the platform in July 1889 at a cost of £15; six years later a cast iron gent's toilet was also provided. In 1904, following the takeover of the Bridport Railway by the Great Western Railway, the original thatched station building and the waiting room and toilet on the platform were removed and a new brick building of a standard GWR design was erected on the platform together with a nearby new station master's house. Following the withdrawal of passenger services on the Bridport to West Bay extension, the 1904 station building remained for many years: in the 1950s and 1960s it was in residential use, 'The Bungalow'. No traces of the station buildings now remain, demolition taking place in the 1970s. Part of the site is now covered by road improvements including a major roundabout, the former alignment of the track bed south to West Bay now followed by Sea Road.

BRIDPORT WEST BAY   SY 465904

Opened: 31st March 1884 (with the opening of the extension of the Bridport Railway to West Bay). *Initial name of Bridport Harbour quickly changed to West Bay.*
Closed: Passengers - Temporary closure 1st January 1916 – 7th July 1919; Final closure – 22nd September 1930 Goods – Temporary closure 1st January 1917 – 7th July 1919; Final closure 3rd December 1962 (very limited subsequent use for movement of coal and shingle until 1st January 1966).

The opening of this station in 1884 was in response to the anticipated development of West Bay as a holiday resort. This was seen as essential following the decline of the harbour as a commercial port, a result of the opening of the railway to Bridport with many sea borne goods, particularly for the net/twine industry, now being imported by rail. The 1884 terminal stone station building on the west side of the line was of a design constructed all over the Great Western Railway. Its early name change from Bridport Harbour to West Bay reflected the resort ambition. Despite the early optimism, West Bay developed slowly as a resort and limited use of the extension from Bridport resulted in the withdrawal of passenger services and closure of the station for passenger traffic in September 1930. Three years later in the summer of 1933 a camping coach was introduced remaining until the outbreak of the Second World War. The station site continued to be used for freight traffic until 1962 and even beyond then until 1966 for the import of coal and export of shingle. Although West Bay closed for passenger traffic over 80 years ago, the building remains today; since closure there have been a series of uses including as a house in the 1930s. In the 1970s the station site was used as a boat yard, the building being the office. After this use ceased the building was boarded up and deteriorated. In the late 1990s, following purchase by West Dorset District Council, the station building was extensively renovated, the only significant structural change being the cutting back of the canopy. Two railway carriages were sited on the track beside the platform and the station building took on a new role as a West Dorset District Council Information Centre, two carriages standing beside the platform. This use ceased in 2001 and the carriages were removed. From the mid-2000s the building has been occupied by a series of cafes and restaurants including the 'Station Diner' when two carriages once again stood by the platform used as dining cars; these were removed in 2008 when this venture failed. The building reopened in 2010 as 'The Tea Station' followed by 'The Station Café' in 2014. When visited in March 2016 the now 'Station Kitchen' served the author and his wife with excellent refreshments. The building was in very good condition and the author was told that the plan is to reinstall carriages alongside the platform on the short section of track that remains in place.

BROADSTONE   SZ 004960

Opened: 2nd December 1872 (as New Poole Junction with the opening of the branch to Poole). Name changes: *New Poole Junction December 1872- January 1876; Poole Junction January 1876 – July 1883; Poole Junction and Broadstone July 1883 – January 1887; Broadstone and New Poole Junction January 1887 – February 1889; Broadstone Junction February 1889 – July 1929; Broadstone (Dorset) July 1929 – 1956; Broadstone 1956 – 7th March 1966*
Closed: Passengers – 7th March 1966 (with closure of the Bath Green Park – Poole line) Goods – 20th September 1965 (some 'carted by public' traffic retained until final closure 7th March 1966).

Opened in 1872, at the junction of the Southampton to Dorchester Railway with the first branch line to Poole, this junction role was reflected in the numerous early names for this station. Increased traffic resulted from the 1886 Corfe Mullen to Broadstone cut off route along which the north/south Somerset and Dorset (S&D) trains by-passed Wimborne. Although some passenger traffic was generated by surrounding residential areas, the principal role of Broadstone station was as an exchange point between passengers on the S&D and trains to Wimborne, Ringwood and Salisbury. It was said that between the arrival/departure of long distance trains the four platforms were virtually deserted. A small goods yard was sited north east of the station. Nothing survives today; the principal station building was dismantled and re-erected at Medstead and Four Marks station on the Mid-Hants Railway (the Watercress Line) in 1984. The whole station site has been redeveloped now occupied by the Broadstone Leisure Centre, its car park and a traffic roundabout. The site's original use is commemorated in the pedestrian/cycle 'Castleman Trailway' running alongside the Centre reflecting the name 'Castleman's Corkcrew' given to the original Southampton and Dorchester Railway. The original 'Railway Hotel' adjacent to the station is now (2016) 'The Goods Shed Free House', an earlier replacement name being 'The Broadstone Hotel'.

CATTISTOCK HALT   SY 594992

Opened: 3rd August 1931 (on the Yeovil – Dorchester line originally opened by the Wilts, Somerset and Weymouth Railway (GWR) in 1857).

Closed: 3rd October 1966.

Opened in 1931 serving the village of Cattistock to the north, the original timber built halt with shelters on both platforms was constructed at an estimated cost of £636. In 1959 the platforms and shelters were rebuilt with Southern Railway style concrete pre-cast sections coincident with the introduction of diesel multiple unit train services. Following the closure of the halt in 1966, the two platforms were transferred for reuse as platforms on the single track line at Chetnole and Thornford both of which are still open in 2016. All other remains of the halt itself have gone, the sole clue to the long closed halt being a small gate by the road underbridge which was the entrance to the down platform.

CHARLTON MARSHALL HALT   ST 897041

Opened: 9th July 1928 (on the Wimborne – Blandford St Mary section of the Dorset Central Railway originally opened in 1860).

Closed: 17th September 1956 (continued to be used until 17th December 1963 by pupils of Claysmore Preparatory School at the beginning and end of each term).

Sited on a double track section and a late addition in 1928 to facilities on the Somerset and Dorset Railway, the halt primarily served the residents of Charlton Marshall village to the south east in the Stour valley. Pupils at the nearby Claysmore Preparatory School also used the halt at the beginning and end of terms. Shelters were never provided on the two short concrete platforms which were linked via steps and the adjacent road bridge. The platforms survive in a reasonable condition, refurbished steps being used by walkers gaining access to the former track bed which now is a section of the Stour Valley Way.

CHETNOLE HALT   ST 598077

Opened: 11th September 1933 (on the Yeovil – Dorchester line originally opened by the Wilts, Somerset and Weymouth Railway (GWR) in 1857).   *Chetnole from 5th May 1969*

Closed: remains open for passenger services on the Bristol – Weymouth line as a request stop.

At its opening in 1933 the halt, costing £410, comprised two oil lit staggered wooden platforms (both 150ft x 7ft)

on the double track line. These were sited either side of a road overbridge from which steps linked to both platforms, the up north of the bridge and down to the south. The original up platform was replaced by the redundant concrete component platform from the former Cattistock Halt when this closed in 1966. Following singling of the line from 26th May 1968 the down platform was demolished.

CHRISTCHURCH   SZ 153932

Opened: First Station – 13th November 1862 (as the terminus of the Ringwood – Christchurch branch from the Southampton and Dorchester Railway; single track extension to Bournemouth East opened 18th March 1870). Second Station – 30th May 1886 (with the doubling of the line to Bournemouth East).

Closed: Passengers – remains open for services on the London (Waterloo) – Weymouth line. Goods – 1st May 1872

The 1862 station was the first rail facility serving the developing town of Bournemouth. East of the current road over bridge, the site is now occupied by modern industrial buildings. The 1886 buildings included the main structure on the down side, two side platforms with large canopies and a covered footbridge at the west end. A goods siding and dock were sited to the east of the station on the down side. These station buildings remain today largely unaltered and in relatively good condition; the footbridge roof has however been removed.

CORFE CASTLE   SY 962822

Opened: 20th May 1885 (with the opening of the Wareham – Swanage Railway).

Closed: Passengers – 3rd January 1972 (with the closure of the Swanage branch line)   Goods – 4th October 1965. Unstaffed: 8th September 1968

Re-Opened: Passengers – 12th August 1995 (on the restored Swanage Railway).

Sited close to the village centre and the famous castle, the station opened in May 1885 with the commencement of services on the Swanage Railway, the only intermediate station between Wareham and Swanage. As such it served not only the village but also much of the Isle of Purbeck. The station was a key factor in attracting visitors to both the castle and the surrounding area, particularly in the pre motor car era. The attractive principal station building on the up side of the line is constructed of Purbeck stone with a roof of red tiles. Including all the main station facilities, the building also incorporated the two storey station master's house the scale of which is indicated by its four bedrooms. On the down platform passengers were served only by a basic waiting shelter. The platforms were linked by foot boards laid across the tracks at both ends; no footbridge was ever built. On the up side at the southern end was a goods shed with small awnings on both sides. A feature of the station for some years was a pair of camping coaches to the rear of the down platform at the Swanage end.

When the line closed in 1972 the station buildings were purchased by Dorset County Council and leased to a computer technology company. When this company ceased trading in 1992 the County Council granted the Swanage Railway a licence to restore the buildings. The station has now been restored to much of its former splendour with its reopening in August 1995 on the Swanage Railway; much of the interior has been restored to its 1950s condition incorporating fittings from other former London and South Western Railway stations. A major achievement was the rebuilding of the signal box on the down platform which had been demolished, following closure in June 1956. The goods shed has been restored as a museum displaying signs and memorabilia relating to the history of railways in Purbeck and Dorset.

CORFE MULLEN HALT   SY 995985
Opened: 5th July 1928 (on the Corfe Mullen – Broadstone cut off single track line originally opened for goods traffic in 1885 and passenger traffic 5th March 1886).
Closed: 17th September 1956.

The opening of this halt in 1928 was a triumph for the residents of Corfe Mullen who had campaigned for it for over 40 years following the commencement of passenger services on the single track cut off in 1886. Sited in a deep cutting, the facilities were basic on the short platform with only a small shelter and one gas lamp. Access was via steps from the adjacent Wimborne – Corfe Mullen road bridge. Following closure of the halt in 1956 the cutting was filled during the 1980s, the site being now beneath the grounds of 112 Wimborne Road. The former track alignment is followed on the north west side of the Wimborne – Corfe Mullen road along the appropriately named 'Corfe Halt Close.'

CORYATES HALT   SY 628847
Opened: 1st May 1906 (on the Abbotsbury branch line originally opened in 1885).
Closed 1st December 1952 (with closure of the Abbotsbury

branch line).

When opened in 1906 on its embankment site 21 years after passenger services commenced on the Abbotsbury branch, the basic facilities comprised a 100ft long platform, 7ft wide and only 14in above track level; passengers needed folding steps to enter and leave the train. Lamps and a name board were provided but no shelter. During the following year the platform height was raised to 3 feet and a GWR pagoda style corrugated iron shelter erected at a cost of £56. In later years a section of the shelter was cut away at the Abbotsbury end so that milk churns could be readily placed in the shade. Patronage was always very limited though on occasions the halt was the destination for excursions such as Sunday School outings. No significant trace now remains but an overgrown mound marks the former site of the platform the edge of which probably survives beneath the undergrowth.

CREEKMOOR HALT   SZ 001941
Opened: 19th June 1933 (on the Broadstone – Poole line originally opened in 1872).
Closed: 7th March 1966 (with closure to passenger traffic of the Bath Green Park – Poole line).

Opened in 1933 to serve the developing local Creekmoor and Waterloo communities, the halt's original platforms constructed of former wooden sleepers were short, only some 2 to 3 carriages long. To serve traffic generated by the nearby RAF factory the wooden platforms were replaced and extended early in the Second World War using concrete components. The original waiting shelters of corrugated metal (down platform) and wood (up) were retained. A small wooden hut acted as a ticket office. Initially there was no footbridge but with the provision of the concrete platforms a concrete 'Southern Railway' style footbridge was erected. The whole station site is now redeveloped, the former track bed being now the alignment of the A 349 Broadstone Way alongside which are industrial units.

DAGGONS ROAD   SU 113125
Opened: 1st January 1876 (on the Salisbury and Dorset Junction Railway, Alderbury Junction – West Moors originally opened 20th December 1866).   *Alderholt until May 1876; Daggens Road until 1904.*
Closed: Passengers and Goods – 4th May 1964 (with closure of the Alderbury Junction – West Moors line).

Serving both Daggons Road and Alderholt, the station

opened nearly eleven years after the opening of the Salisbury and Dorset Junction Railway through the site. The main buildings, including the station master's house, a booking office and ladies' room were on the up (towards Salisbury) platform; their architectural style differed from other stations on the line, no platform canopy being provided. Today a residential cul-de-sac serves the station site on the north side of the B3078 where Station Road changes to Daggons Road. The former station master's house, 'The Old Station Cottage' survives in residential use, the former track bed filled to platform level. Alongside are three new houses on the former station site: 'The Old Waiting Room'; 'The Sidings' and 'Buffers'. The former road overbridge immediately to the south of the station has gone.

DORCHESTER SOUTH   SY 692900

Opened: 1st June 1847 (as the western terminus of the Southampton and Dorchester Railway). *Dorchester until 26th September 1949*

Closed: Passengers – remains open for services on the London (Waterloo) – Weymouth Line. Goods: 1st March 1965 (with the concentration of goods traffic at Weymouth though some 'carted by public' traffic retained until 1st December 1980).

There have been greater changes in the passenger facilities at this station than at any other Dorset station. The first 1847 station was the western terminus of the Southampton and Dorchester Railway aligned east – west at a site south of the town, an alignment reflecting the company's ambition to extend the line further west towards Exeter. This extension was strongly opposed both by local residents and the Great Western Railway which in 1857, through its subsidiary the Wilts, Somerset and Weymouth Railway, cut across this proposed extension at right angles with the opening of the Yeovil – Dorchester – Weymouth line. From this north/south line a single track curved link line ran from south of the newly opened Dorchester (later West) station to just east of the Southampton and Dorchester station.

The alignment of the original 1847 line and the 1857 curve dictated the layout of the station for many years. A single long platform with a cross over facility at the midpoint initially served both up and down trains, a common arrangement at many early stations when the town was located principally on one side of the station (eg. Taunton). At an early stage a second shorter platform parallel to the original long was added mainly serving down trains. With these arrangements through up and down

trains serving Weymouth were required to undertake reversing movements to access both platforms. Following the 1878 doubling of the Weymouth spur, a new down platform on the inside of the spur was constructed coming into use on 4th May 1879 making the short down platform redundant. Up trains from Weymouth still however needed to reverse into the continuing up platform. A subway was later constructed linking the new curved down platform and this original up platform. A timber train shed covered the original lines and the subsequent short down platform; a wooden canopy covered the up platform. Passengers on the 1879 curved down platform were served by a timber shelter. In 1937/8 the old train shed and the long redundant short down platform were removed and a new canopy was erected on the main station building as a part of a general renovation. Thirty two years later in 1970 there was a further major change with the provision of a new up platform with a waiting room and shelter on the outside of the Weymouth link curve. The principal buildings on the original old up platform remained in use and an elevated walkway was constructed across the old trackbed to the new up platform. After another 17 years a new station building was constructed alongside the 1970 curved up platform incorporating a waiting room and booking office; a separate shelter was also provided all coming into use on 21st November 1987. The 1879 curved down platform was also rebuilt, the timber shelter being replaced by a small brick and metal structure; a new footbridge was also constructed. Soon after the original 1847 station building was demolished and the site incorporated within the adjacent brewery complex with the platform structure surviving for some years. Throughout all these changes to the station buildings a large goods shed stood east of the station on the up side and an engine shed also east of the station on the down side.

Over the last 25 to 30 years, the station has operated with the layout and facilities largely as introduced in 1987. By contrast some twenty five associated railway buildings north and west of the station including the goods shed have been demolished associated with a series of redevelopment schemes the largest and most extensive of which is still in progress. When used by the author in October 2015, Dorchester South station was dominated by the phase one (completed) and phase two (under construction) of the major 'Brewery Square' development. The sites of the former engine shed and associated sidings has been redeveloped for housing.

DORCHESTER WEST SY 689902

Opened: 20th January 1857 (with the opening of the Yeovil – Weymouth section of the Wilts, Somerset and Weymouth Railway (GWR)). *Dorchester until 26th September 1949*
Closed: Passengers – remains open for services on the Bristol – Weymouth line Goods – 1st March 1965 (coal traffic retained until 6th September 1965). Unstaffed: 2nd January 1972

The original principal building on the down side, in the style of the Wilts, Somerset and Weymouth Railway, is considered to be the best surviving example of that company's architecture. Passengers travelling first and second class were provided with separate waiting rooms; for some years a Wyman's bookstall served the down side passengers. The original building on the up platform, linked to the down platform by a footbridge at the north end, was rather limited but early in the twentieth century, reflecting increasing passenger numbers a new building was erected. In 1908 both platforms were extended northwards and the down platform was widened. A feature of Dorchester West from its early days was a fine wooden overall roof covering both platforms; this was removed in 1934 and replaced by glazed canopies on both platforms. Extensive facilities for handling goods traffic evolved over the years south of the station particularly on the down side. They included the former stone built broad gauge goods shed, traders' sidings and cattle pens. There was competition with the freight facilities at Dorchester South which eventually took over as the dominant goods station because of its superior links with the London area. In the early 1970s the up side main station building was demolished being replaced by a small brick shelter. In February 1989 an article in the Daily Telegraph described Dorchester West as 'one of the country's worst railway stations'. Today, the situation is much improved. The original building on the down platform, now listed as of historical and architectural importance, survives but none of the interior is in railway use; when seen in October 2015 most of the rooms were occupied by a Domino's Pizza restaurant. The footbridge and sections of the early railings remain in place. The goods yard has been redeveloped with industrial/warehouse units.

EASTON SY 690718

Opened: Passengers – 1st September 1902 Goods – 1st October 1900 (as the terminus of the Easton and Church Hope Railway).
Closed: Passengers – 1st March 1952 (with closure of the Weymouth – Portland – Easton line to passenger traffic).

Temporary closure 11th November 1940 - 1st January 1945 but open for summer service 1941 – 1944.   Goods – 5th April 1965.

The 1902 building, in a cutting close to the centre of Easton, comprised a single 300 foot long platform with a local stone building which incorporated a booking hall, a general waiting room, a ladies' room and toilets. This original building was destroyed by fire on 28th November 1903 but rebuilt in its original form May – September 1904. An unusual feature was a collection of fossils collected from the cutting and nearby quarries displayed on the platform. Further items were displayed in glass fronted cases within the station. Passenger services were curtailed during the Second World War. A small goods yard with a goods shed was sited south of the station. Easton closed for passenger services in 1952 but remained in use for goods traffic for a further 13 years. The station building survived for some years minus its canopy; following demolition the whole site was redeveloped by the Council as elderly persons accommodation (Ladymead); this use was continuing when seen in late 2015. The road bridge at the northern end of the site carrying Reforne Street is still in place.

EVERSHOT ST 593042

Opened: 20th January 1857 (with the opening of the Yeovil – Weymouth section of the Wilts, Somerset and Weymouth Railway (GWR)).
Closed: Passengers – 3rd October 1966   Goods – 7th September 1964. Unstaffed: 7th September 1964

Located some 500ft above sea level, Evershot station opened in January 1857 when services commenced between Yeovil and Weymouth. It was sited at Holywell, a cross roads and group of houses about a mile east of the village of Evershot. An unusual feature was that a number of the local gentry, in particular Lord and Lady Ilchester, had the right to have any passenger train stop at the station. The station buildings, the main building on the up side (towards Yeovil) and the shelter on the down, were unusual on the Wilts, Somerset and Weymouth Railway in being constructed of timber. A footbridge at the southern end originally featured an ornate roof. A goods yard was sited south of the station on the up side; cattle pens were served by a short siding behind the up platform. Alterations over the years included platform lengthening in 1913/14. Until the mid-1940s the station had its own station master; in the 1950s there were two porters and three signalmen but Evershot became unstaffed from September 1964 when goods facilities ceased. Following demolition in 1967 there are today very few remains aside from isolated posts and railings; a row of railway cottages survives.

GILLINGHAM   ST 810261

Opened: 2nd May 1859 (as the temporary western terminus of the Salisbury and Yeovil Railway; the extension on to Sherborne opened on the 7th May 1860).

Closed: Passengers – remains open for services on the London (Waterloo) – Exeter line   Goods – 5th April 1965 (except private siding fertiliser traffic).

Opened in May 1859 it was, for almost a year, the western terminus of the Salisbury and Yeovil Railway, the extension on to Sherborne being completed early in May 1860. The main station building was, and continues to be, a fine example of the architecture of Sir William Tite who designed many station buildings across southern England. On the up side of the line, incorporating accommodation for the station master and the principal station facilities, it originally featured slate hung walls to prevent damp but these were later removed. A brick shelter was sited on the down platform. The initial footbridge was open; this was replaced in 1967 by a concrete structure from Dinton station in Wiltshire which had closed for passengers in March 1966. A large goods shed stood in a goods yard west of the station on the up side. For many years the area surrounding Gillingham station/Station Road was the hub of local business and industry including a brick and tile factory to the south and a bacon factory to the north. The original main building, when visited in late 2015, was largely unaltered, the 'No.One café' providing refreshments for the author at the eastern end. A metal and glass shelter serves passengers on the down platform replacing the earlier brick structure. The former goods yard is the station car park.

GRIMSTONE AND FRAMPTON   SY 641943

Opened: Passengers – 20th January 1857 (with the opening of the Yeovil – Weymouth section of the Wilts, Somerset and Weymouth Railway (GWR)).   Goods – October 1905. *Frampton until July 1857; Grimstone until about July 1858.*

Closed: Passengers – 3rd October 1966. Goods – 1st May 1961. Unstaffed: 11th April 1966.

Opening for passengers with the line in 1857, the station served the villages of Grimstone to the south west and Frampton to the north west. Goods facilities were not provided until 1905. Following doubling of the track in the mid-1880s, the station had two platforms linked by an open footbridge; the brick structures comprising the principal building and gents' toilet were on the down (towards Dorchester) platform and a waiting shelter on the up. Fine ornate lamps were provided on both platforms. The station buildings were demolished in 1967; limited traces of the bases of the platforms and buildings remain today particularly on the down side. The former goods yard is occupied by an oil distribution depot accessed only by road.

HAMWORTHY   SZ 004901

Opened: 1st June 1847 (as the terminus of the Poole Junction – Poole branch from the Southampton and Dorchester Railway   *Poole until 2nd December 1872).*

Closed: Passengers – 1st July 1896 (with closure of the Hamworthy branch for passenger traffic).   Goods – 2nd March 1981 (date of formal closure but the branch continues in use for limited freight traffic).

This was the first station serving Poole from which passengers travelled on to the town by a toll bridge or ferry. Its role declined with the opening of the direct branch line from New Poole Junction (later Broadstone) to Poole in 1872 and all passenger services ceased in 1896. The branch line has remained in use for limited freight traffic serving the harbour and private sidings; the station building has been demolished but the platform remains.

HAMWORTHY JUNCTION   SY 987918

Opened: 1st June 1847 (at the junction of the Southampton and Dorchester Railway and the branch line to the first Poole station)   *Poole Junction until 2nd December 1872. Renamed Hamworthy 1st May 1972.*

Closed: Passengers – remains open for services on the London (Waterloo) – Weymouth line   Goods – 20th September 1965.

Sited at the junction of the Southampton and Dorchester Railway with the branch line that ran south to the first Poole station, the original buildings were demolished in 1892. They were replaced in 1893 (coincident with the opening of the Holes Bay curve) by a side platform on the up side, on which stood the principal building, and a down island platform with a waiting shelter. There were canopies on both platforms with wind breaks on the up, pedestrian movement between the platforms being through a subway at the Poole end which also acted as a link between two residential areas, Turlin Moor and Hamworthy itself. The Station Master's house stood beside the up side building at the Poole end but has now gone. The down side building was demolished in 1972, replaced by a shelter with a flat roof and the outer platform on the south side is now disused and fenced off. The 1890s up side brick building remains today, disused and with a shortened canopy; on the down side a 1998 arch roof metal and glass shelter was used by the author when visiting in October 2015. The subway continues to be used by passengers and local residents. The signal box which controlled movements between the main line and the branch, sited at the Poole end of the down platform, has been demolished.

HARMANS CROSS   SY 983800

Opened: March 1989 (as the terminus of the Swanage Railway until the opening of the extension to Corfe Castle and Norden in 1995).
Closed: remains open for services on the Swanage Railway.

A two platform station, Harmans Cross is sited on a curved loop which acts as the main crossing point for trains on the Swanage Railway. A new signal box with a local stone base and wooden cabin has been constructed to an original LSWR design.

HERSTON HALT   SZ 015793

Opened: Easter 1984 (as the first terminus of the Swanage Railway).
Closed: remains open as a request stop on the Swanage Railway.

A simple wooden platform sited alongside a loop line, it was superseded as the terminus of the Swanage Railway in 1989 with the opening of Harmans Cross station.

HOLTON HEATH   SY 946902

Opened: 3rd April 1916 (on the section of the Bournemouth – Weymouth line originally opened by the Southampton and Dorchester Railway in 1847). Passenger station only. Originally for use only by workers at the adjacent works; general public use from 14th July 1924.
Closed: remains open for services on the London (Waterloo) – Weymouth line. Unstaffed: 1st June 1964

Opened in 1916 to serve workers at the nearby Royal Navy cordite factory which was operational 1914 – 1961, the station only became available for general public use in 1924. The original waiting shelters on both platforms were replaced by very small metal and glass shelters which remain today as does the original open footbridge.

LAKE HALT   SY 988906

Opened: 1916 (on the Hamworthy Junction – Hamworthy branch line originally opened in 1847.
Closed: c.1918/9

The halt was built in 1916 (twenty years after regular passenger services ceased on the line) on an embankment by the low bridge over Lake Road. This short lived halt served special train services conveying workers at a nearby wartime Admiralty shipyard. At the end of hostilities the halt closed and was later demolished.

LYME REGIS   SY 334926

Opened: 24th August 1903 (with the opening of the Axminster and Lyme Regis Light Railway).
Closed: Passengers – 29th November 1965 (with the closure of the Lyme Regis branch).   Goods – 3rd February 1964.

Lyme Regis was the terminus station of the last passenger line opened in Dorset in 1903. The single platform with a bay (added in 1906) was sited on the up (west) side of the single track line approximately a half mile from the town centre, a location determined by the fact that beyond the southern end of the site the land falls steeply towards the sea. A feature of the predominately wooden station building was the attractive fretted canopy edge. A northern extension to the building was used for some years as a W H Smith kiosk and subsequently as a store; by 1936 it had lost its end windows and was later removed to St Mary Cray station in Kent. The platform was reconstructed in the late 1920s by the Southern Railway; a new SR style name board omitted any reference to Charmouth included for some years on the previous version. The goods shed initially stood beyond the station at the southern end of the site on the east side. It was later dismantled and re-erected opposite the north end of the station platform.

After the 1965 closure of the branch line, the station building lay derelict for over 14 years. In early 1979, the Mid Hants Railway (the Watercress Line) removed much of the surviving building and re-erected it as a gift and bookshop at Alresford station. Following purchase by the local authority, the whole site has been redeveloped with warehousing and light industrial units including, as at many South West former station sites, a builders merchant. At the far north end of the former station site is the Lyme Regis Medical Centre. When visited in November 2015, these uses continued to occupy the former station site with no trace of the station buildings.

MAIDEN NEWTON   SY 599979

Opened: 20th January 1857 (with the opening of the Yeovil – Weymouth section of the Wilts, Somerset and Weymouth Railway (GWR)).

Closed: Passengers – remains open for services on the Bristol – Weymouth line.   Goods – 5th April 1965 (some 'carted by public' facilities retained until 18th April 1966). Unstaffed: about April 1971.

In addition to serving Maiden Newton itself and the surrounding rural areas, the station at the east end of Station Road was at the junction between the Yeovil to Weymouth line and the Bridport Railway on which services commenced some 11 months after the main line. This main line was initially single track with Maiden Newton a crossing point, as today after the lifting of the second track in 1968. Following the doubling of the tracks in the early 1880s, the station comprised two platforms serving the main line and a terminal bay on the up side at the northern end for use by trains on the Bridport branch. Knapped flint structures included the main station building with a long canopy on the up platform incorporating the principal offices and a waiting shelter on the down; the bay track was partially covered by a timber train shed. For much of its life a lattice style footbridge linked the platforms but this was replaced by a Southern Railway style concrete structure recycled from a closed station on the Salisbury – Exeter line. A large stone, flint and timber goods shed, originally built for use by broad gauge trains, was sited on the up side at the Dorchester end of the site. Before the Second World War the scale of activity at Maiden Newton for both passenger and freight traffic is indicated by the staffing level of a station master plus at times up to eleven other staff. Today the up side main building remains. In recent years it has had various uses, in early 2000 as an IT Training Centre. When visited in early 2016 it was however not occupied. On the down platform the original shelter remains. Metal structures housing the token keys allowing use of the single track lines north and south of the station are sited at the northern end of the up platform and the southern end of the down. The branch line track bed has been filled in and now is a footpath. Remnants of the early gates and railings at the station can be seen but the goods shed and cattle pens have gone.

MELCOMBE REGIS   SY 678796

Opened: 30th May 1909 (on the Weymouth and Portland Railway originally opened in October 1865). Passenger station only.

Closed: 3rd March 1952 (with closure of the Weymouth – Portland line for passenger traffic). Date of closure for Portland line trains; remained in use as a regular relief platform for Weymouth station until 12th September 1965 and occasionally thereafter.

When services commenced in 1865 on the Weymouth to Portland line trains had to reverse into and out of Weymouth station as the junction of the main line and the Portland branch, a short distance north of Weymouth station faced south. When a new bridge was constructed in 1908 over the Backwater replacing the 1864/5 wooden structure the opportunity was taken to erect this new station on the embankment leading to the new bridge. Opened in mid-1909, it comprised a 400 ft. long timber platform on the down side of the single track. The building's initial canopy was small but was subsequently replaced by a larger pitched structure. A distinctive feature was the later large iron screen on the Backwater side of the line to protect waiting passengers from the wind. The platform was rebuilt with stone blocks in the 1930s. Behind the platform a set of tank traps was constructed during the Second World War; these remained in place for many years after the War. Although formally closed in 1952, the station continued in regular use as a relief platform for Weymouth station until September 1965 and occasionally thereafter. The station building was demolished in the mid-1960s but the concrete platform survived for a further twenty years. The northern end was demolished in 1985 during the construction of the roundabout (now a junction) at the west end of King Street; the remainder was demolished during the development of the retirement/sheltered housing 'Swannery Court' in 2000. Thus no trace of the station now survives.

MEYRICK PARK HALT   SZ 077926

Opened: 1st March 1906 (on the Bournemouth – Poole line originally opened in 1888).

Closed: 1st November 1917.

The halt opened in 1906 three quarters of a mile west of Bournemouth Central station to serve what was then a growing residential area. Two short platforms with huts were mainly used by local steam rail-motor services which had been introduced to compete with local tram services. It was connected to the southern end of Meyrick Park Crescent by two flights of steps on the embankment. It closed in 1917 as a war time economy measure and never reopened being demolished in 1919. No trace can now be seen. The site can be identified by a wider section of the embankment east of the rail bridge over Meyrick Park Central Drive.

MONKTON AND CAME HALT   SY 683883
Opened: 1st July 1905 (on the Dorchester – Weymouth section of the Wilts, Somerset and Weymouth Railway (GWR) originally opened in 1857). *Came Bridge Halt until 1st October 1905.*
Closed: 7th January 1957.

This timber built halt with two platforms opened with the commencement of local steam rail-motor services between Dorchester and Weymouth. It principally served golfers at the nearby Came Down Golf Club but was also used by residents of the nearby village of Winterborne Monkton; hence the second name 'Monkton and Came Halt.' The platforms were subsequently rebuilt with concrete components; there was limited lighting with oil lamps but platform shelters were never provided. The two platforms survive nearly sixty years after the halt closed in 1957.

MORETON   SY 779891
Opened: 1st June 1847 (With the opening of the Southampton and Dorchester Railway).
Closed: Passengers – remains open for services on the London (Waterloo) – Weymouth line. Goods – 1st March 1965 (coal traffic continued until 20th September 1965). Unstaffed: 1st March 1965.

Opened in 1847 with the commencement of services on the Southampton and Dorchester Railway, the station principally serves the village of Moreton about a mile to the east and Crossways to the south. The original main building on the up (towards Wareham) side featured an impressive gable and intricate canopy. An unusual feature of the original down side shelter was the series of elliptical arches beneath the very narrow canopy facing the tracks. Over time extensions were added to the up side building including a number related to the operation of the adjacent small goods yard on the up side. The platforms were extended twice: first in 1970 to take four car units and then in 1988 with the introduction of longer electric trains on the London (Waterloo) to Weymouth services. The original buildings on both platforms have now been replaced with small metal and glass shelters. To the rear of the up platform are 'Station Cottages' The original signal box sited beyond the level crossing east of the station on the up side was closed and demolished following the introduction of automatic barriers.

NORDEN   SY 956828
Opened: 12th August 1995 (as the terminus of the reopened Swanage Railway)
Closed: Remains open as the terminus of the Swanage Railway

Acting in the role of a 'park and ride' facility for passengers on the Swanage Railway, the car park has a capacity of some 300 cars. The booking office is in an old LSWR crossing keeper's hut relocated from East Stoke on the Waterloo to Weymouth main line and restored by the Swanage Railway.

PARKSTONE   SZ 037915
Opened: 15th June 1874 (with the opening of the Poole – Bournemouth West extension of the Broadstone – Poole branch).
Closed: Passengers – remains open for services on the London (Waterloo – Weymouth line).   Goods – 20th September 1965 (date of final closure but much of the goods traffic had been transferred to Poole in about 1953).

The only intermediate station when the Broadstone to Poole branch was extended east to Bournemouth West in 1874, the initial modest buildings were soon expanded into a substantial facility serving Parkstone and Branksome. For some years the platform sign stated 'Parkstone for Sandbanks'. The principal building on the up side incorporated accommodation for the station master; a substantial wooden shelter stood on the down platform. The up and down platforms were originally provided with canopies though of different design indicating different construction dates. On the up side platform wind breaks at both ends of the canopy provided extra shelter. A fully glazed footbridge was erected in 1888. Houses were erected on the down side goods yard south of the station after its 1965 closure. The main up side building with the canopy is still in place; the down side platform has only a small metal and glass shelter. The platforms are linked at the west end by the now open footbridge, the roof/glazing having been removed in the early 1950s.

POKESDOWN   SZ 124924
Opened: 1st July 1886 (on the Christchurch – Bournemouth East (later Central) extension of the Ringwood – Christchurch line opened in 1870). Passenger station only.
Pokesdown 1886 – 1891; Pokesdown (Boscombe) 1891 – 1897; Pokesdown 1897 – 2009 (for a period 1930-late 1940s Pokesdown for eastern Bournemouth); Pokesdown

for Boscombe (from 16th May 2009).

Closed: remains open for services on the London (Waterloo) –Weymouth line.

The first station opened following a long campaign by Boscombe/Pokesdown residents, the name changes over the years reflect on-going local pressures. The 1886 facilities, accessed by a long flight of steps from an entrance on the road bridge east of the station, comprised a long island platform on which stood a waiting room, station offices and a small signal box. The quadrupling of the rail tracks resulted in a complete rebuild of the station in the years 1930/1, the island platform being replaced by two side platforms accessed from a new station entrance on Christchurch Road. Today the station remains generally as in this 1930s re-building.

POOLE   SZ 013911

Opened: 2nd December 1872 (as the terminus of the New Poole Junction (later Broadstone) – Poole branch line from the Southampton and Dorchester Railway).

Closed: Passengers – remains open for services on the London (Waterloo) – Weymouth line.   Goods – 18th July 1966.

Three buildings have served as Poole station during its over 140 year history. The first station adjacent to the town centre opened in 1872 as the terminus of the branch line from New Poole Junction (later Broadstone). Sited on a sharp curve, facilities gradually developed as routes served by the station increased, in particular the through route to London via Bournemouth, Brockenhurst and Southampton (1888) and the more direct route to Dorchester and Weymouth via the Holes Bay embankment (1893). From 1893 Poole station was thus on two through routes: Bath – Bournemouth West (Somerset and Dorset Railway) and London (Waterloo) – Weymouth (London and South Western Railway). Brick buildings with large canopies served passengers on both curved platforms, the principal facilities being on the down side. There was a large goods yard with a substantial goods shed on the up side north east of the station, this closed early in 1972. The first station buildings were demolished in 1969 with the construction of the Towngate road bridge over the station site, being replaced by a featureless 'clasp' type structure behind the Wareham end of the up platform. In 1988 this inadequate structure was replaced by another building, again on the up side, the principal feature being a vaulted roof suspended by four columns. Two shelters were provided on the down platform, the platforms linked by an open footbridge. These 1988 facilities continue to serve passengers.

PORTESHAM   SY 604855

Opened: 9th November 1885 (with the opening of the Abbotsbury Railway).

Closed: Passengers and Goods – 1st December 1952 (with closure of the Abbotsbury branch).

Sited on the south side of the line, the local stone building was a good example of the William Clarke station design found at other stations on the branch and across many parts of the South West. Similar to other stations of this design, access to the building was only via the platform and a wooden gate alongside. The single platform on the down side was 223ft long paved with granite slabs beneath the canopy and loose gravel elsewhere. The limestone building with a hipped roof, three tall chimneys and a wide canopy incorporated a general waiting room separated from the booking office by a wooden partition, a ladies' waiting room, store, lamp room, coal store and toilets. A roof light in the canopy enhanced lighting in the waiting room. During the 1930s a GWR camping coach stood on a short siding at the Abbotsbury end of the station. A small goods shed was sited directly opposite the station building. Like Abbotsbury station Portesham was a popular destination for Sunday School excursions from Weymouth, the nearby fields being ideal for games and picnics. During the mid-1960s the station building was converted into a house and today is used for holiday letting with the appropriate name of 'Sleepers'. The former goods shed has been refurbished and the old loading gauge remains.

PORTLAND   SY 682741

Opened: First Station 16th October 1865 (as the terminus of the Weymouth and Portland Railway). Second station 7th May 1905 (on the Easton and Church Hope Railway originally opened for passenger traffic in 1902).

Closed: Passengers – 2nd March 1952 (with closure of the Weymouth – Portland - Easton line to passenger traffic). Goods – 5th April 1965.

The 1865 station, at the northern end of Victoria Square, comprised a basic single platform with a stone building across the end of the track. With a number of developments under way in Portland Harbour passenger numbers increased greatly (in 1865 291,349 tickets were sold at the station) and conditions became very cramped; the need for improvements increased further with the opening in 1902, for passenger traffic, of the line to Easton. To serve this new traffic a temporary wooden platform was provided on the Easton line linked to the 1865 building by a footpath, an arrangement that continued for three years though on occasions for a limited period the 1865 building continued to receive passenger trains. The building functioned as a goods depot until demolition in February 1969 with the construction of the new Victoria Square roundabout.

The second through station on the line to Easton opened in 1905, the down platform on the 2nd February and the up (towards Weymouth) on the 7th May. The original timber platforms were later replaced by Southern Railway stone and concrete components. The 500ft long platforms were linked by a fully enclosed footbridge. The buildings, incorporating waiting rooms and toilets, were constructed of brick, corrugated iron and wood; lightweight materials were required, the station being on land originally reclaimed from Portland Harbour. The second station, constructed some six feet higher than the 1865 structure which had been prone to flooding affecting Victoria Square, was damaged in an air raid on the 11th August 1940 and demolished in April 1954. The site has been completely redeveloped; for some years it was occupied by the Royal Naval Air Station, HMS Osprey at the entrance to which was a plaque recording the 1905 Portland station.

PORTLAND NAVAL HOSPITAL PLATFORM   SY 685813
Opened: c.1925 (on the Portland – Easton line opened for passenger traffic in 1902).
Closed: c.1965

This 60 ft. platform on the south side of the single track line served the nearby Royal Naval Hospital. At the east end of the platform a girder bridge carried the Easton line over the Merchants' Railway incline.

POWERSTOCK   SY 522953
Opened: 12th November 1857 (with the opening of the Bridport Railway, Maiden Newton – Bridport). *Poorstock until about 1862.*
Closed: 5th May 1975 (with closure of the Bridport line).
Goods – 13th April 1961.   Unstaffed: 11th April 1966

Sited in the hamlet of Nettlecombe south east of Powerstock, the station was the only intermediate station on the Bridport branch when it opened from Maiden Newton to Bridport in 1857. On the up side of the line the station building, mainly constructed of stone, incorporated the station master's house and the usual facilities. In 1910 the platform was lengthened. Behind the station building was a small goods yard with two short sidings and a loading platform. For a short time from 1936 a six berth camping

coach was sited at the station. Although passenger trains continued to stop at Powerstock until 1975, the station building was sold in November 1968. The building was modernised including a loft with windows overlooking the main track bed and the goods yard; the passenger recess at the rear of the platform was incorporated into the house now named 'The Old Station'. A section of the platform remains; the former track bed has been grassed over as part of a large lawn.

RADIPOLE HALT   SY 674811
Opened: 1st July 1905 (on the Dorchester – Weymouth section of the Wilts, Somerset and Weymouth Railway (GWR) originally opened in 1857). *Radipole from 5th May 1969*
Closed: 6th February 1984 (official closure date but no trains had called after 31st December 1983 for safety reasons).

Opened with the introduction of a local steam rail-motor service between Dorchester and Weymouth in 1905, the aim of the halt was to serve this developing suburb of Weymouth. It initially comprised two wooden platforms with GWR style cast iron pagoda shelters behind. These platforms were replaced in 1949 by concrete slabs mounted on pre-cast concrete slabs; the pagoda huts were retained; in the 1960s these were painted black. In August 1974 electric lighting replaced the original gas lights and in June 1977 glass and metal shelters replaced the pagoda huts. The halt was formally closed in early February 1984 but no trains served it after the 31st December 1983 as the structure was declared unsafe. When seen in early 2016 no trace was evident apart from the line of the path leading to the down platform and a section of old railings adjacent to the Spa Road bridge, a sad sight for the author who used Radipole Halt frequently in his young days and remembers its use for instance by children travelling to the schools in Dorchester.

RODWELL   SY 675784
Opened: 1st June 1870 (on the Weymouth and Portland Railway originally opened in 1865). Passenger station only.
Closed: 2nd March 1952 (with the closure of the Weymouth – Portland line to passenger traffic).

A single 100ft long platform opened in 1870 on the then single track line through a deep cutting to serve the nearby developing residential area. On the platform was a small stone building, incorporating a booking office and ladies waiting room, and the first small signal box.; this platform was extended in January 1894. A loop line and new upside platform with a GWR pagoda style shelter and new signal box was added from 8th December 1907; at this time the main down side building was enlarged and a lattice type footbridge erected. The main building was destroyed during an air raid on 15th April 1941 which killed the sole staff member on duty. The building was not rebuilt being replaced by a concrete hut. Following closure of the station in 1952, with the withdrawal of passenger services on the Weymouth – Portland line, the tracks remained in use through the site for goods traffic until 1965, the tracks being lifted in 1969/70. There was no goods yard or shed as Rodwell station was not accessible by road vehicles. Today the former track bed is used by the Rodwell Trail, a cycle/pedestrian path along a section of the Weymouth – Portland line from Westham to Wyke Regis. The two platforms survive together with a Trail sign indicating the former site of Rodwell station. When seen in October 2015 the former up platform was covered in vegetation but the down platform was fairly clear; the path to the down platform from Wyke Road was still there used by cyclists and walkers to access the popular Trail.

SANDSFOOT CASTLE HALT   SY 675774

Opened: 1st August 1932 (on the Weymouth and Portland Railway originally opened in 1865).

Closed: 2nd March 1952 (with closure of the Weymouth – Portland line to passenger traffic).

The halt opened in 1932 to serve both local residents and visitors to the nearby Sandsfoot Castle and Castle Cove responding to the concern that the use of the Portland line was being adversely affected by the bus services. The basic facilities comprised a 300ft cinder surface platform faced with old sleepers containing solid ash filling on which was a small wooden shelter. For a short period a footbridge provided safe access for the nearby Southlands estate residents. A small section of the platform, together with a sign, survives alongside the former trackbed now used by the Rodwell Trail, a cycle/pedestrian path along the former Weymouth – Portland line. Old railway sleepers have been bolted on to the main surviving section. Further remnants of the platform can also be glimpsed in the undergrowth towards Rodwell station.

SHERBORNE   ST 641162

Opened: 7th May 1860 (as the western terminus of the extension of the Salisbury and Yeovil Railway from Gillingham) further extension of the line to Yeovil opened on 1st June 1860.

Closed: Passengers – remains open for services on the London (Waterloo) – Exeter line.   Goods – initial closure 5th April 1965, some 'carried by public' traffic until final closure 18th April 1966.

For almost a month in May 1860 Sherborne was the western terminus of the Salisbury and Yeovil Railway whose original plan was to locate north of the town. The final route passed to the south after the owner of Sherborne Castle withdrew his objection with the stipulation that two fast trains a day should always stop at the station. A fine example of a Sir William Tite design, the building, constructed in stone from the nearby Ham Hill quarry, stood behind the up platform incorporating the station master's house and the main facilities. A covered footbridge was added in 1886 though unusually it was unglazed. Facilities on the down side have changed over the years; the original 1860 shelter was replaced by an arched structure in 1926 but was superseded by a shelter and large canopy in 1962. Modern lighting facilities replaced the Southern Railway light standards during the 1980s. The introduction of the Class 159 trains on the line brought a number of minor improvements. The station is today generally in the form following the 1962 changes, including the original 1860 Tite building on to which a small extension has been added at the west end accommodating the gents' toilets. Facilities at the station, when visited by the author and his wife in January 2016, included the excellent Station Café. The former goods yard west of the station on the up side is now a car park; the goods shed is in commercial use (in early 2016 as 'The Railway Shed' and 'Ace Fibreglass' Sherborne Ltd). Beyond the level crossing at the east end of the station two signal boxes operated over the years, an 1875 box on the down side and its 1960 replacement on the up side, the latter closed on the 4th January 1970 and has now been demolished. At one time in the 1980s it was available for let as an office.

SHILLINGSTONE   ST 824117

Opened: 10th September 1863 (with the opening of the Blandford St Mary – Blandford – Templecombe section of the Somerset and Dorset Railway).

Closed: Passengers – 7th March 1966 (with closure of the Bath Green Park – Poole line to passenger traffic).   Goods: 5th April 1965.

Sited at the northern end of the mile long village, the station also served Child Okeford and Okeford Fitzpaine.

The original 1863 main red brick building with cream decorative brickwork around the windows and a welsh slate roof served passengers on the up (towards Sturminster Newton) platform. Modifications undertaken during the early days of the 20th century included the addition of the station master's office and a canopy. It is thought that this canopy was erected because the station was used by King Edward VII who as Prince of Wales went shooting at the nearby Iwerne Minster House. At its opening there was only a single track through the station alongside which was the later up platform; in 1878 a second track, passing loop and down platform with shelter were added. A signal box was erected to control the passing loop. Beyond the northern end of the up platform was the goods yard.

Following closure of the goods yard in April 1965 and of the station in March 1966 with the withdrawal of passenger services, the track was lifted through the site between March and May 1967; the down side shelter and signal box were demolished but the main station building was spared and today is the only station in Dorset built by the Dorset Central Railway to survive. The principal reason for survival was its use by a number of light industries but by the end of 1998 the station was derelict.

The County Council purchased the track bed for future use as a section of the proposed Shillingstone by-pass; by the end of 2002 the by-pass plan had been abandoned and the Council decided to dispose of the now unoccupied station buildings. Following protracted negotiations, the North Dorset Railway Trust took over the lease which was finally signed at the end of June 2005. In anticipation of this the Trust commenced work on a restoration programme in late 2003, the aim being to restore the station to its appearance in the early to mid-1950s. The main building has now been renovated and opened to the public in 2008 including a shop and café, the latter serving hot coffee to the author and his wife during their visit on a cold day in February 2016. Toilets are also provided, the gents including the original cast iron urinals! The track bed to the north and south of Shillingstone is now a section of the North Dorset Trailway; at the station the Trailway runs along the former down platform. The signal box has been rebuilt and opened in October 2011; level crossing gates have been installed at the southern end of the platforms and in February a shelter was being erected on the down platform in the style of the original based on the original foundations. The former goods yard is now used as a car park associated with the St Patrick's Industrial Estate developed alongside the former station approach road. A restored former second class MK 1 SK carriage acting as an overflow café was alongside the up platform in February 2016 and nearby were two 0-6-0 austerity tank locos very recently arrived for restoration.

SPETISBURY   ST 913021
Opened: 1st November 1860 (with the opening of the Wimborne – Blandford St Mary section of the Dorset Central Railway). *Originally 'Spetisbury' downgraded to a halt 13th August 1934.*
Closed: 17th September 1956.   Unstaffed: 13th August 1934

Sited adjacent to and slightly above the south west edge of the village, the 1860 station was on a then single track section of the Dorset Central Railway with a booking office and waiting room on the only platform. Following doubling of the line in 1901, new larger scale buildings were erected on the new up platform including a booking office, waiting room and toilets. The original buildings on the now down platform were replaced by a shelter. Originally classed as a station, Spetisbury was downgraded to a halt from 13th August 1934. The buildings were demolished in 1958/9 but the two platforms and a section of the main building rear wall survived. The station site is being renovated by the 'Spetisbury Station Project' and evidence of this was clear when visited on the 10th March 2016. The aim of the Project as stated on a notice is 'To authentically restore the Platforms and 1901 Station Building to house a Visitor Centre and Café'.

STALBRIDGE   ST 739181
Opened: 10th September 1863 (with the commencement of services on the Blandford St Mary – Blandford – Templecombe section of the Somerset and Dorset Railway – formal opening 31st August 1863).
Closed: Passengers – 7th March 1966 (with the closure of the Bath Green Park – Poole line for passenger traffic). Goods – 5th April 1965.

Located less than a mile north east of the town centre, the brick station buildings, of a typical Dorset Central Railway design, were principally on the up (towards Templecombe) platform. They included the station master's house, the booking office and signal box. A small shelter stood on the down platform. There was no footbridge; the pedestrian link between the platforms was via a board crossing at the southern end of the station immediately adjacent to a level crossing. A small goods yard on the up side a little to the north of the station building included a goods shed and cattle pens. The down platform and shelter, the signal box and booking office were demolished in 1967; the station house and up platform survived a further 5 years in a derelict state. The station site and goods yard were then redeveloped and today a large industrial unit (William Hughes) and car park occupy the whole area. A hump in Station Road indicates the line of the former level crossing; just to the west rail tracks across the road are remains of a former goods line which passed through the goods shed, extended during the Second World War to serve a Ministry of Food depot. To the east is 'The Sidings' development of small industrial units not on the site of the former sidings.

STOURPAINE AND DURWESTON HALT ST 860091
Opened: 9th July 1928 (on the Blandford St Mary – Blandford – Templecombe section of the Somerset and Dorset Railway originally opened in 1863).
Closed: 17th September 1956.

A late addition to passenger facilities on the Templecombe to Blandford section of the Somerset and Dorset Railway, this halt serving Stourpaine to the north and Durweston to the south west opened sixty five years after services commenced on the line. A short 120ft long concrete platform on concrete stilts stood on top of an embankment adjacent to a bridge over a farm track. A small concrete shelter was added some years after the opening. Today some remnants of the platform can still be seen on the embankment but the shelter has gone.

STURMINSTER NEWTON   ST 789141
Opened: 10th September 1863 (with the commencement of services on the Blandford St Mary – Blandford – Templecombe section of the Somerset and Dorset Railway – formal opening 31st August 1863).
Closed: Passengers – 7th March 1966 (with the closure of the Bath Green Park – Poole line for passenger traffic). Goods – 5th April 1965.

Sited close to the town centre the red brick station buildings were typical examples of the Dorset Central Railway design. The principal buildings on the up (towards Stalbridge) platform included separate waiting rooms for ladies and gentlemen, the booking office and station master's office. Passengers on the down platform were served by a small wooden shelter with a fretted canopy. The platforms were slightly staggered, the up platform extending slightly further west and the down a little to the east; in the centre of the up platform a dip led down to a wooden board crossing to the west end of the down platform, there being no footbridge. A wooden signal box stood at the east end of the up platform. To the north of the station on the down side a goods yard included a small brick goods shed. For many years a nearby weekly cattle market generated much traffic. The station buildings were demolished in the early 1970s; roads and a large car park now cover the station site while the former goods yard is occupied by commercial buildings. A section of the former cutting west of the station was infilled in the early 1990s to form an open space close to the town centre. In 1992 gates were installed at the southern end at the instigation of the Somerset and Dorset Railway Trust incorporating the words 'Somerset and Dorset Joint Railway'. A plaque alongside the gates states "Here passed the engines and men of the Somerset and Dorset Railway closed 6th March 1966". In 2007 the open space was modified into its current state as 'The Railway Gardens'. All that remains of the station facilities is a former storage building, now Streeters carpet shop, on the north side of Station Road. Beyond the east end of the station site the former track bed is followed by the North Dorset Trailway to Blandford which also passes through Shillingstone station.

SWANAGE   SZ 029789
Opened: 20th May 1885 (with the opening of the Swanage Railway, Wareham – Corfe Castle – Swanage).
Closed: Passengers – 3rd January 1972 (with the closure of the Swanage branch line).   Goods – 4th October 1965. Partially unstaffed 8th September 1968.
Re-opened: 1975 (licence to use the station site granted by the Council); 1979 (operations over a short length of track commenced).

The 1885 station building in the centre of Swanage on Station Road incorporated the station master's house at the west end and the usual facilities. There was a relatively short platform and canopy. The buildings and platforms were extensively rebuilt and extended in 1937/38 with a longer platform canopy; the new facilities included a parcels office, ticket office, a waiting hall and newsagents shop. This rebuilding in Purbeck stone blended well with the retained station master's house. Significant parts of this rebuilding used Southern Railway type concrete components including the platform, fences and lamp posts. The introduction of the last unfortunately resulted in the loss of the fluted barley sugar style lamp posts, a feature of the original station. Another feature of

Swanage station for many years was the large Benn and Cronin metal indicator showing train departure times.

The advent of the restored and reopened Swanage Railway from 1975 led to a major refurbishment of the station buildings including early work on the canopy and the reinstatement of the bay platform which had been filled in. The main station building is now used by the Swanage Railway including the booking office and book/gift shop (the former parcels office); also incorporated are offices for the Wilts and Dorset bus company and a taxi firm. The former station master's house is occupied by offices relating to the Swanage Railway. Alongside the front of the station are a number of bus stops, a sign over the station entrance says 'Swanage Travel Interchange'. Much of the large former goods yard south of the station is today occupied by a supermarket, with a large car park. In the former station yard opposite the station building is the Swanage Medical Practice. The former large goods shed west of the station (extended in 1898 and 1937) has been restored and is used by the Swanage Railway for carriage restoration and maintenance. Also in current use are the small locomotive shed west of the station and the turntable. At the far east end of the site a former carriage serves as a part of the Birds Nest Café.

THORNFORD BRIDGE HALT   ST 593125
Opened: 23rd March 1936 (on the Yeovil – Weymouth section of the Wilts, Somerset and Weymouth Railway (GWR) originally opened in 1857). *Thornford Bridge from 5th May 1969; Thornford from 6th May 1964*
Closed: remains open for services on the Bristol – Weymouth line as a request stop.

Sited about one mile south west of the village of Thornford, the halt opened some 80 years after services commenced on the Yeovil to Weymouth line. The halt originally had two staggered timber platforms (150ft x 7ft) on the then double track line separated by a road bridge from which there was access via steps to the platforms (up platform to the north, down to the south). Small wooden shelters lit by oil lamps stood on both platforms. The original wooden up platform and shelter were replaced by a concrete platform and shelter transferred from Cattistock Halt when this closed in 1966; these remain in use today. The down wooden platform and shelter were demolished following their disuse when the line was singled on 26th May 1968. In 2016 trains only stop by request.

TOLLER   SY 563978
Opened: 31st March 1862 (on the Bridport Railway originally opened in 1857).
Closed: Passengers – 5th May 1975 (with closure of the Bridport line).   Goods – 4th April 1960.   Unstaffed: 11th April 1966.

The station opened five years after services commenced on the Bridport Railway. For some thirty years no shelter was erected on the platform but, responding to complaints, a small hut was then provided. Following a fire in 1902, significant improvements came in 1905, a Great Western style wooden building being erected on the platform lengthened at the east end. Also added was a cast iron gent's urinal, a facility at many rural stations. At the same time the original down side goods siding was extended and converted into a loop and a small loading dock was provided which handled considerable local traffic, in particular the handling of milk churns. In 1981, six years after the station closed, members of the then Dart Valley Railway Association dismantled the building and it was re-assembled in June 1986 on a new platform at what is now Totnes Littlehempston, the southern terminus of the South Devon Railway where it is now the main station building housing the booking office and waiting room. A large part of the Toller platform survives: the west end is a section of a public footpath that crosses the track bed at the foot of the ramp; a section of the station iron railings remains.

UPWEY   SY 671840
Opened: 21st June 1871 (on the Dorchester – Weymouth section of the Wilts, Somerset and Weymouth Railway (GWR) originally opened in 1857). Passenger station only. *Station appears to have been mis-spelt 'Upway' for a few weeks after opening.*
Closed 19th April 1886.   Replaced by Upwey Junction

Following the start of services on the Dorchester to Weymouth line in 1857, the residents of Upwey and Broadway campaigned for a local station. Thirteen years later in 1870 the GWR agreed on the condition that the local residents contributed £150 towards the cost; in response £174.2s.0d was raised (Upwey residents £83.18s.6d; Broadway residents £90.3s.6d). This first Upwey station, believed to be of timber construction, was actually sited in Broadway just to the north of the railway bridge spanning what is now known as Old Station Road. With the opening of Upwey Junction station about a half mile to the south at a point where the Abbotsbury branch left the main line, the station closed and by October 1887 had been demolished though it is thought that that one of its shelters was transferred to the down platform of the new Junction station. No trace of this first Upwey station remains though its site is still indicated in the road name. It is unique being the only Dorset station of which no photograph is known to exist.

UPWEY (ABBOTSBURY BRANCH) SY 667836

Opened: 9th November 1885 (with the opening of the Abbotsbury Railway). *Originally opened as 'Broadway' (then Broadwey from June 1891), it was re-named Upwey on 1st January 1913 to avoid confusion with Broadway station in Worcestershire.*

Closed: Passengers – 1st December 1952 (with closure of the Abbotsbury branch to passenger and goods traffic beyond Upwey).   Goods – 1st January 1962. *Renamed Upwey Goods 1st December 1952.*

Opened in 1885 with the commencement of services on the Abbotsbury branch, the station was on the south side of the single track line. The local stone building, designed by William Clarke like others on the branch and a number of others across the South West, was constructed by a local builder from Broadway, Edwin Snook. An unusual feature was the roof of red and blue tiles alternating every third row. Before the Second World War a GWR camping coach stood on a short siding at the west end of the platform. West of the station was a large stone goods shed and south of this a siding served local coal merchants. Following closure of the branch in 1952, the building suffered, the already shortened canopy being removed in 1955. Goods traffic continued on the short section of the branch to the main Dorchester – Weymouth line (designated as a goods siding), the building being renamed Upwey Goods. Sold by auction on the 24th September 1968 the site was redeveloped, the station building being incorporated in industrial premises, a situation which was continuing when seen in early February 2016, the occupiers being 'Buildrite Trade and DIY Supplies'. The former goods shed is in commercial use in part as a 'cash and carry collection point'.

UPWEY JUNCTION   SY 671832

Opened: 19th April 1886 (on the Dorchester – Weymouth section of the Wilts, Somerset and Weymouth Railway (GWR) originally opened in 1857). Passenger station only. *Renamed Upwey and Broadway 29th November 1952; renamed Upwey 12th May 1980.*

Closed: remains open for services on the London (Waterloo – Weymouth and Bristol – Weymouth lines. Unstaffed: 1st March 1965

At the point where the Abbotsbury branch line left the main Dorchester – Weymouth line this junction station opened in April 1886 five months after the Abbotsbury services commenced acting both as a transfer point and a service for local residents replacing the closed original 1871 Upwey station. During the First World War extra traffic was generated by the nearby Australian army camp. An unusual feature of the station was the varying levels of the adjacent up main and branch platforms, the up serving trains climbing towards Bincombe Tunnel and the branch serving trains beginning their rapid descent towards Abbotsbury. The platforms were level at the Weymouth end of the station but were significantly different at the northern end, a stone wall separating them. The branch platform also acted as the final section of the approach road to the main station.

The principal wooden building was on the up main platform, the station master's office, booking office, waiting room and toilets all opening onto this platform access to which was by steps from the branch platform. Narrow canopies on either side of the building gave some cover for waiting passengers, in the case of those on the branch platform minimal, the canopy being high above the platform. The original small waiting room on the down platform was of a different style to that on the up; it is thought to have been transferred from the first Upwey station. In 1923 the down platform was reconstructed. Use of the branch platform ceased in 1952 with closure of the Abbotsbury line; some 30 years later in 1986 the track bed was filled in using rubble from the old Weymouth station and a new car park was constructed. The original buildings were demolished in 1972 and subsequently the structures were revamped including modern metal and glass shelters and a renovated footbridge. These facilities serve services both on the Bristol line and the electric trains on the London – Weymouth line which in 2016 call hourly at the now Upwey station which had been named Upwey and Broadwey until 12th May 1980 after it ceased to be a junction station in 1952.

UPWEY WISHING WELL HALT   SY 672852

Opened: 28th May 1905 (on the Dorchester – Weymouth section of the Wilts, Somerset and Weymouth Railway (GWR) originally opened in 1857).

Closed: 7th January 1957.

Opened with the commencement of local steam rail-motor services between Dorchester and Weymouth in 1905, the initial facilities were two wooden platforms behind which stood corrugated iron GWR style pagoda huts. In 1946 these huts were replaced by precast concrete huts on the rebuilt concrete platforms. Illumination was provided by oil lamps. The principal role for the halt, indicated by its name, was conveying tourists to and from the Wishing Well in Upwey village, though this was sited over a mile below the halt. Increasing competition in this role from cars and buses which could take passengers very close to the well and its distance uphill from the village and the steep access steps which deterred use by Upwey residents led to the halt's early closure in January 1957. The author recalls war time stories from his father who, when in the Home Guard during the Second World War, undertook duties based at the halt guarding the nearby Bincombe Tunnel. The redundant platforms remained in place for some years but no trace of them could be seen when travelling through the site in early 2016.

VERWOOD   SU 077093

Opened: 20th December 1866 (with the opening of the Salisbury and Dorset Junction Railway, Alderbury Junction – West Moors).
Closed: Passengers and Goods – 4th May 1964 (with the closure of the Alderbury Junction – West Moors line).

One of four original intermediate stations, each with a passing loop on this generally single track line, the station principally served Verwood but two nearby brickworks also generated goods traffic from incoming coal and outgoing brick products. The main station building, including a canopy stood on the up (towards Salisbury) platform beside which, to the south was a signal box. There was only a shelter on the down platform. The small goods yard on the up side south of the station incorporated cattle pens. The station facilities remained largely unaltered throughout its near one hundred year life. Unusually a public house, the Albion Hotel, stood in the station yard behind the main building. The former station site is now redeveloped occupied by a realigned section of the B3081 road (now south of the Albion Hotel) and housing (Albion Lane). The original road overbridge and a short section of the old road remain to the north of the Hotel, the bridge disused.

WAREHAM   SY 919882

Opened: First Station 1st June 1847 (with the opening of the Southampton and Dorchester Railway). Second Station 4th April 1887 (larger station providing improved interchange facilities with the Swanage Railway opened in 1885).
Closed: Passengers – remains open for services on the London (Waterloo – Weymouth line). Goods – 4th May 1970 (small siding remained in use for oil products traffic until December 1978, small goods transferred to Poole in about 1951).

The first Wareham station, opened in 1847 with the commencement of services on the Southampton and Dorchester Railway, was sited east of the present station and the pre-1980 level crossing. Alongside the crossing on the down side was the station master's house and beyond this was the goods yard with a goods shed. Partly to provide improved facilities for passenger exchange with the 1885 Swanage branch, a new station was constructed west of the level crossing in 1886 (the date shown high up on the down side building) and opened in April 1887. Bay platforms on both the up and down sides were principally used by the Swanage line trains. The level crossing east of the station was replaced on 3rd April 1980 by a new road bridge. Significant renovation was undertaken in 1988 and in the late 1990s and Wareham is now seen as a fine example of a surviving London and South Western Railway station. A visit in October 2015 showed that rooms in the downside building were occupied by 'Cyclexperience', a one stop bike hire and repair shop.

WESTHAM HALT   SY 676793

Opened: 1st July 1909 (on the Weymouth and Portland Railway originally opened in 1865).
Closed: 2nd March 1952 (with closure of the Weymouth – Portland line to passenger traffic).

The halt, adjacent to Abbotsbury Road just to the south of the Littlefield level crossing, opened with the introduction of the local steam rail-motor service on the Weymouth – Portland line. The platform on the up (Westham) side of the single track was originally faced with timber and on the platform was a wooden shelter; the platform was lengthened in 1913. In the 1890s a signal box was built on the down side from which the level crossing gates were operated by a wheel. As the pedestrian activity grew in the surrounding area, a subway was completed on the north side of Abbotsbury Road in August 1922. The platform was rebuilt in July 1946 with a stone face; an iron shelter with a flat roof replaced the wooden structure. Beside the entrance gate on Abbotsbury Road was a small wooden hut for the ticket collector who attended at peak times, for instance in the early morning and late afternoon when Westham Halt was used extensively by pupils attending the nearby Weymouth Grammar School travelling to and from homes on Portland and in the Rodwell and Wyke areas. The 1946 platform survives today at the northern end of the Rodwell Trail which uses the former track bed of the Weymouth – Portland line from Westham to Wyke Regis

WEST MOORS   SU 080030

Opened: 1st August 1867 (on the Southampton and Dorchester Railway originally opened in 1847).
Closed: Passengers – 4th May 1964 (with the closure of the Ringwood – Broadstone and Alderbury Junction – West Moors lines to passengers).   Goods – 20th September 1965 (some army specials until 1974).

This junction station opened eight months after services began on the Salisbury and Dorset Junction Railway which joined the Southampton and Dorchester Railway just north east of the station. At that time the local population was small but this subsequently increased greatly to the south particularly around Ferndown. The importance of the station for Ferndown was reflected in the station signboard 'West Moors for Ferndown'. The principal building was on the up (towards Ringwood) platform; a wooden shelter served passengers on the down platform. A concrete footbridge was erected in the 1900s. There were goods sidings on both the up and down sides, on the up side the siding was partly behind the platform. In 1943 the station became the location of a war time petrol depot. The signal box stood on the up side adjacent to and east of a level crossing.

The station site is now redeveloped with elderly persons housing (Castleman Court); the Castleman Trail passes through the site. The name 'Castleman' refers to the nickname for the Southampton to Dorchester Railway 'Castleman's Corkscrew', because of its winding alignment. The house formerly occupied by the operator of the level crossing gates survives as 'Gatemans Cottage' on the south west side of the B3072 opposite the station site. Reference to railway history is also seen in the name of the adjoining public house 'The Tap & Railway' (superseding the earlier 'Railway Hotel').

WEYMOUTH   SY 679796

Opened: Passengers – 20th January 1857 (as the southern terminus of the Wilts, Somerset and Weymouth Railway). Goods – 2nd March 1857.
Closed: Passengers - remains open for services on the London (Waterloo) – Weymouth and Bristol – Weymouth lines. Goods – 14th August 1972

Weymouth's increasing role as a resort following the earlier royal patronage of George III together with its growth as a cross Channel port led to great demands in the town for a link to the county's developing rail network. Eventually the Wilts, Somerset and Weymouth Railway (a subsidiary of the GWR) opened for passengers in January 1857 providing services to Yeovil, Bristol, the Midlands and London (Paddington) via Chippenham. In addition a new spur at Dorchester introduced a link to the Southampton and Dorchester Railway (absorbed by the London and South Western Railway) which had opened to the county town 10 years earlier; this permitted through services to the resort from London (Waterloo). These services by the two companies brought complications for the track layout at the new station with the GWR services running on broad gauge and the LSWR services on standard; this situation was resolved in 1874 with the removal of the broad and mixed gauge tracks.

The 1857 terminus station close to the Esplanade, built on reclaimed land, included a sub-structure of trussed timber resting on a large number of timber piles. The timber station with an overall roof and glazed end screens was built by a local builder T.Dodson for some £10,000. The design was based on working drawings provided by J.H. Bertram, one of Brunel's chief assistants and engineer of the GWR for eight months after Brunel's death. The whole complex including the station, engine sheds, goods facilities and tracks cost some £44,000. At its opening the glazed overall roof spanned two platforms and tracks and three centre sidings. On either side of the main roof were shorter covered bay platforms. By 1890 the station was fully developed but, although built and owned by the GWR, it operated for some years as a joint station. Not only were specific platforms used by the two companies but until 1914 the London and South Western Railway appointed its own station master and staff; from that year the GWR took over responsibility for the whole station complex.

Between the two World Wars Weymouth grew in popularity with holiday makers; many excursions arrived from all over the country, in particular those from the GWR works at Swindon during the original 'Swindon Week' and later 'Swindon Fortnight'. This increasing traffic generated demands for improved and expanded facilities; a 1909 scheme was not implemented but limited work was undertaken in the late 1930s. As a safety precaution the roof glazing was removed in 1939 and the overall roof structure was dismantled 12 years later in 1951. In 1956/7 partial rebuilding included the construction of a 950 ft. long island platform on the Ranelagh Road side. Finally nearly 130 years after its opening the original largely wooden structure was demolished commencing on the 13th August 1984. The new station came into use on 3rd July 1986; the 1957 platform was incorporated and a new platform constructed for use by the trains on the Bristol line opened in July 1987. In the mid-1980s the tracks in the area were electrified and the new London (Waterloo) – Weymouth electric service began on 16th May 1988. Today the station, as completed in 1986, continues in full operation, including half hourly weekday services to London. The sole remnant of the 1857 structures is the substantial stone wall bordering Ranelagh Road.

Over the years extensive freight facilities were provided at Weymouth including a very large goods shed, yard and siding complex west and north of the station; the yard closed in August 1972. In recent years much of this area has been redeveloped as a retail park and for other commercial uses. The goods shed, which was used as an amusement arcade for a spell after closure in 1972, was demolished during the redevelopment. Some three quarters of a mile north of the station on the down side an extensive yard incorporating sheds and repair facilities evolved serving both Great Western and Southern Railway locomotives. It was extensively damaged in the Second World War. By 1970 virtually all the yard had been cleared and was subsequently redeveloped for housing.

WEYMOUTH QUAY   SY 684788
Opened: Passengers – 4th August 1889 (with the opening of the Weymouth station - Weymouth Quay tramway to passenger services). Goods - 16th October 1865 (with the opening of the Quay tramway to goods traffic).
Closed: Passengers – 26th September 1987 (with the closure of the Weymouth Quay tramway to scheduled passenger services). Temporary Closure for passenger services: 6th September 1939 – 15th June 1946 Goods – 1st March 1972. Last train used the station on 2nd May 1999.

The 1889 station was a single platform attached to the quay buildings for use by boat trains from London travelling along the tramway from Weymouth station.

These basic facilities were replaced from 13th July 1933 when major improvements including two platforms costing some £120,000 were opened by the Prince of Wales. Passenger services were suspended during the Second World War. A third platform was added in 1961 and during the early 1960s four to six boat trains used this quay station on summer Saturday. A new quay building opened in 1972 but use of the third 1961 platform ceased. The boat train services ceased in September 1987 but the buildings continued in use for some years by passengers for continuing ferry services to the Channel Islands. These too have now ceased and when seen in early 2016 the quay building and north end of the platform remained in place but unused.

WIMBORNE   SZ 01899
Opened: 1st June 1847 (with the opening of the Southampton and Dorchester Railway).
Closed: Passengers – 4th May 1964 (with the closure of the Ringwood – Broadstone line to passenger traffic).   Goods – 28th February 1966 (some 'carted by public' traffic until final closure 2nd May 1977).

Remarkably Wimborne station could claim in the 1860s and 1870s to be the most important station in Dorset. Opened originally in 1847 when services commenced on the Southampton and Dorchester Railway, its importance increased when services from Bath to Poole started through Wimborne in 1863 on the Somerset and Dorset Railway. However with the completion of the 'coastal route' from Southampton to Weymouth via Bournemouth and Poole in 1893 and also the opening of the Corfe Mullen cut-off for passengers in 1886 eliminating through north/south movements, the important 'cross roads' role of Wimborne ceased and decline set in leading to its eventual closure for passenger services in 1964, an event which would have seemed unbelievable a century before.

The station was on a curve, a significant factor in the operation of passenger and freight traffic generated both by its exchange role and the local population and businesses. Facilities changed as the roles of the station evolved; the original down platform became an island platform in the late nineteenth century and subsequently two bay platforms were added although the down bay was not used after April 1938. The up bay was downgraded to a goods siding in 1933. Both platform canopies were extended early in the twentieth century and a separate building was redeveloped as a refreshment room. A number of flat roofed extensions were added over the years. A particular feature of the station was a tall signal box at the north end of the up platform. There were significant goods facilities at the station including the goods yard containing a large goods shed on the down (east) side and cattle pens to the west behind the up bay. The station and goods yard site were cleared by July 1983 and earth works were undertaken to reduce parts of the site down to the surrounding road level. The site is now redeveloped and occupied by the Riverside Business Park; the former station use is indicated on a plaque on the side of a unit close to the entrance. The previous use is today also reflected in the continuing nearby road names 'Station Road' and 'Station Terrace.'

WOOL   SY 844869

Opened: 1st June 1847 (with the opening of the Southampton and Dorchester Railway).
Closed: Passengers – remains open for services on the London (Waterloo) – Weymouth line. Goods – 1st March 1965.

Through its long history since its opening on the Southampton and Dorchester Railway Wool station has served a variety of customers: residents in the village and surrounding rural areas, visitors to the Dorset coast (for many years the station name board stated 'Wool for Lulworth Cove') and the military based at Bovington Camp and the nearby tank and gunnery ranges to the south. The main station building and a shelter were sited on the down side (towards Dorchester) platform; in 1969 these were replaced by a featureless prefabricated structure. The original wooden shelter on the up platform has been replaced by a metal and glass structure. For a period in the 1960s two Pullman camping coaches stood behind the up platform. Today the 1969 building and modern shelter continue to serve passengers.

WYKE REGIS HALT   SY 669765

Opened: 1st July 1909 (on the Weymouth and Portland Railway originally opened in 1865).
Closed: 2nd March 1952 (with closure of the Weymouth – Portland line to passenger traffic).

Opening in 1909 with the commencement of steam rail-motor services to Portland, its primary role was to serve the nearby Whitehead & Co. torpedo works (later Wellworthys) which had opened in the late 19th century. On the up (west) side of the single track line the initial facility was a wooden platform with a GWR pagoda style shelter.

Concrete components were introduced in February 1913 with the lengthening of the platform; this was required to serve extra traffic generated during the First World War by increased activities at the torpedo factory. It was estimated that on some occasions over 1000 workers were using the halt each day. An additional flat roofed hut was added in 1930 and further rebuilding took place in 1946 including a concrete platform. Closed with the withdrawal of passenger services on the Portland line in 1952, very limited remnants of the concrete section survive in the undergrowth alongside the track bed which has a new role as a section of the Rodwell Trail which runs from Wyke Regis to close to Weymouth town centre at Westham. Alongside the trail signs have been erected indicating the station and halt sites; unfortunately when walking the Trail in October 2015 the author could only glimpse a small section of the sign in the undergrowth which also entirely covered the platform which largely survives.

YETMINSTER   ST 597108

Opened: 20th January 1857 (with the opening of the Yeovil – Weymouth section of the Wilts, Somerset and Weymouth Railway (GWR)).
Closed: Passengers – remains open for services on the Bristol – Weymouth line as a request stop.   Goods – 5th April 1965.   Unstaffed: 6th October 1969

The station has served the village and the surrounding rural area for nearly 160 years, much of the traffic involving short work and shopping trips to and from Yeovil. The original Wilts, Somerset and Weymouth Railway style main buildings were on the up (towards Yeovil) platform. A stone waiting shelter served passengers on the down platform behind which was the station master's house. Pedestrian movements between the platforms were via steps and the road overbridge at the south end of the station. A small goods yard on the up side north of and behind the station served a coal merchant and small animal feed warehouse; an additional siding for a United Dairies depot was added in 1932. Following singling of the line through the station all trains now use the former up platform   passengers being served by a metal and glass shelter; trains stop only by request. The brick built former station master's house is in residential use; the former down platform survives but largely hidden by undergrowth, nearby is the Railway Inn.

FURTHER READING

Atthill R., *The Somerset and Dorset Railway*, David and Charles, 1967

Butt R.V.J., *The Directory of Railway Stations*, Patrick Stephens Ltd, 1995

Clark R.H., *An Historical Survey of selected Great Western Railway Stations – Layouts and Illustrations Vol 2* Oxford Publishing Co., 1979 Vol 3 Oxford Publishing Co., 1981

Clinker C.R., *Register of Closed Passenger Stations and Goods Depots 1830-1977*, Avon Anglia, 1981

Cox J.G., *Castleman's Corkscrew – The Southampton and Dorchester Railway 1844-1847*, City of Southampton, 1975

Dale P., *Dorset's Lost Railways*, Stenlake Publishing, 2001

Deacon T., *The Somerset and Dorset: Aftermath of the Beeching Axe*, Oxford Publishing Co., 1995

Gosling T. and Clement M., *Dorset Railways*, Sutton Publishing, 1999

Gough T., The Southern - West of Salisbury, Oxford Publishing Co., 1984

Gough T. and Mitchell D., *British Railways Past and Present No 29 Dorset, No 44 Dorset A Second Selection*, Past and Present Publishing Ltd, 1996 and 2004

Hawkins M., *Somerset and Dorset Then and Now*, David and Charles, 1995
    LSWR West Country Lines Then and Now, David and Charles, 1993

Haysom D. and Parker J., *The Last Days of Steam in Dorset and Bournemouth*, Alan Sutton, 1993

Jackson B.L., *The Abbotsbury Branch*, Wild Swan Publications Ltd, 1989
    Isle of Portland Railways, Vol 2, Oakwood Press, 2000

Jackson B.L. and Tattershall M.J., *The Bridport Branch*, Oxford Publishing Co., 1976
    The Bridport Railway, Oakwood Press, 1998

Judge C.W. and Potts C.R., *Somerset and Dorset Railway: An Historical Survey of Track Layouts and Illustrations*, Oxford Publishing Co., 1979

Kidner R.W., *Railways of Purbeck (Revised)*, Oakwood Press, 2000
    Southern Railway Halts, Oakwood Press, 1985

Lucking J.H., *Railways of Dorset*, Railway Correspondence and Travel Society, 1968
    Dorset Railways, Dovecote Press, 1982
    The Weymouth Harbour Tramway, Oxford Publishing Co., 1986

Lund B. and Laming P., *Dorset Railway Stations on Old Picture Postcards*, Reflections of a Bygone Age, 2005

Maggs C.G., *Branch Lines of Dorset*, Sutton Publishing, 1996 Amberley Publishing, 2013
    Dorset Railways, Dorset Books, 2009
    The Bath to Weymouth Line, Oakwood Press, 1982

Mitchell V. and Smith K., Middleton Press (Various publications dates)
    Bournemouth to Evercreech Junction, 1987
    Bournemouth to Weymouth, 1988
    Branch Line to Lyme Regis, 1987
    Branch Line to Swanage, 1986 and (Revised), 1999
    Branch Lines around Weymouth, 1989
    Branch Lines around Wimborne, 1992
    Salisbury to Yeovil, 1992

Southampton to Bournemouth, 1987

    Yeovil to Dorchester (including Branch Line to Bridport), 1992

Nicholas J. and Reeve G., *Main Line to the West Part 2 - Salisbury to Yeovil*, Irwell Press, 2007

Oakley M., *Discover Dorset - Railway Stations*, Dovecote Press, 2001

Oppitz L., *Dorset Railways Remembered*, Countryside Books, 1989

Peters I., *The Somerset and Dorset*, Oxford Publishing Co., 1984

Phillips D., *Westbury to Weymouth Line*, Oxford Publishing Co., 1994

Phillips D. and Pryer G., *Salisbury to Exeter Line*, Oxford Publishing Co., 1997

Phillips D., *Salisbury to Exeter – The Branch Lines*, Oxford Publishing Co., 2000

Popplewell L., *Bournemouth Railway History*, Dorset Publishing Co., 1973

Potts C.R., *An Historical Survey of selected Great Western Stations – Layouts and Illustrations Vol. 4*, Oxford Publishing Co., 1985

Pryer G.A. and Bowring G.J., *An Illustrated Survey of selected Southern Stations – Track Layouts and Illustrations Vol 1*, Oxford Publishing Co., 1980

Quick M.E., *Railway Passenger Stations in England, Scotland and Wales*, RCMS 2nd Edition 2003, Supplement 2005

Robertson K., *GWR Halts Vol 1*, Irwell Press, 1990

    GWR Halts Vol 2, KRB Publications, 2002

Smith M., *Railways of the Isle of Portland*, Irwell Press, 1997

Stone C., *Rails to Poole Harbour*, Oakwood Press, 1999

Thomas D.StJ., *Regional History of the Railways of Great Britain – The West Country*, David and Charles, 1981

Vaughan A., *A Pictorial Record of Great Western Architecture*, Oxford Publishing Co., 1977

Wright A.P.M., *The Swanage Branch – Then and Now*, 1992

Young J.A., *Main Line to Bournemouth (Revised Edition)*, Bournemouth Local Studies, 1991

    The Ringwood, Christchurch and Bournemouth Railway (Revised Edition), Bournemouth Local Studies, 1992

ACKNOWLEDGEMENTS

The majority of the 'Then' photographs reproduced in this book are from:

The **Colin Caddy collection**: Pages 13(top), 15(middle), 16(bottom), 21(bottom), 23(top & bottom left), 26(middle), 27(top left & middle), 30(top), 31(top), 32(middle), 39(middle), 41(top), 43(middle), 44(middle left), 46(top left & middle), 47(top), 49(middle), 51(bottom right), 53(top), 55(middle), 57(top), 58(top), 59(bottom left), 60(top), 61(top left & right), 62(middle), 64(top left & middle), 68(middle left and bottom left), 69(middle), 70(top), 71(middle), 73(bottom left), 74(top), 75(top).

The **Lens of Sutton collection**: Pages 13(top & middle), 16(top), 18(top), 19(top), 20(top), 21(top), 22(top), 25(top), 26(bottom left), 28(top), 32(top), 34(top), 35(middle), 37(top & bottom left), 38(top), 42(top), 44(top), 45(top), 47(middle), 48(upper middle), 49(top), 52(bottom), 54(middle left), 56(middle), 59(middle), 60(middle), 63(top), 65(top), 66(top & middle left), 67(top), 73(top middle), 74 (upper middle), 77(top).

Also from the collections of **RK Blencowe**: Pages 23(middle), 24(middle left) and **Colin Maggs**: Pages 40(top), 72(top).

The author is grateful for the permission given for their use.

The remaining 'Then' photographs are from the author's collection or where the copyright is unknown or unclear. All the 'Now' photographs (2015/2016) were taken by the author.